# SEALING THE TESTIMONY

# SEALING THE TESTIMONY

## AN EYEWITNESS ACCOUNT OF THE MARTYRDOM

# TED GIBBONS

Maasai, Inc.
Provo, Utah

Published by Maasai, Inc.
201 East Bay Blvd
Provo, Utah 84606

Front cover graphic design by Douglass Cole, Orem, Utah.
Page Layout and Design by www.SunriseBooks.com

A video tape presentation of the testimony of Willard Richards is
available. It is entitled *I Witnessed the Carthage Massacre*. It was
made on location at Carthage Jail, and features Ted Gibbons as
Willard Richards. Address orders and inquiries to:

W.R. Enterprises
124 West 400 South
Orem, UT 84058
or call (801) 226-2797

1988 edition by Keepsake Books. Formerly entitled, *I Witnessed
the Carthage Massacre*.
ISBN: 0-99985-06-0
2001 edition by Maasai, Inc.
Library of Congress Card Number: 2001116251
ISBN: 0-9708008-4-3

10  9  8  7  6  5  4  3  2  1

*For*
*Mike and Jerry*
*Who taught me to teach.*

## Other Titles by Ted Gibbons

AMEN! An Interrupted Prayer
Brigham Young and the Robin Soup
Daniel Webster and the Blacksmith's Fee
Lincoln and the Lady
The Samaritan
The Talking Cat
Rending the Veil of Heaven
Misery and Joy
This Life is a Test
I Witnessed the Carthage Massacre video and audio cassette
The Road to Carthage

# TABLE OF CONTENTS

# INTRODUCTION

One ought never to begin a book with an apology, so call this a warning. *Not everything you read in this book is factual.*

I have researched the lives of Joseph Smith and Willard Richards for almost three decades now and have studied every document I could find that has a bearing on their relationship and their involvement in the martyrdom at Carthage. In that process I have come to know some things about Willard Richards and his feelings for the Church and for its first prophet, the incomparable Joseph Smith. With those feelings and the background of literally thousands of hours of study and research, I have tried to tell this story in an appropriate way. I am confident that I have read everything Doctor Richards ever wrote about Joseph Smith and the martyrdom. In addition I have read a multitude of records of other eyewitnesses to the events of the Spring and Summer of 1844. I have made a live presentation of the material in this book about 1400 times since I first became Willard Richards for my seminary class on February 4th of 1974.

Even so, in a effort to portray the majesty of Joseph Smith—his life, his power, his death—from the point of view of Willard Richards, I have discovered gaps in the history—places in need of transition material in order to maintain the continuity of the account. I have shamelessly created such material when needed in order to maintain the flow of the narrative. In most cases the reader, unless he or she is well-grounded in this area of Church history, will not know where such material has been inserted. That is because I have tried in every instance to make these insertions true to the characters of Willard and those around him. I have spoken the words I believe they might have spoken, and described the things they might have done when they were in the circumstances portrayed.

But please do not use the language of this work as a primary document in your study of Church history. Not all the words are Willard's words. Not all the events transpired exactly as I have described them. The footnotes are perfectly reliable and can be studied with confidence. But the works from which those notes come, and other sources on the affairs in Hancock county in 1844, must be the place from which you derive your most reliable data on these events.

If you are interested in an entirely factual account of the events of the martyrdom, the wicked men and the traitors together with their motives and machinations, consider a volume I have written as a companion to this work, *The Road to Carthage*. That book is as accurate as my research can make it.

Having said all of that, let me here assure the reader that this book is *true*. It is true to the characters of Joseph Smith and Willard Richards. It is true to the sequence of events as they transpired. It is true to the intimacy between Joseph and Willard.

One day I hope to meet Doctor Richards. If by the grace of the Son of God I should one day have the opportunity to be in this good man's presence, I suspect that we will eventually get around to talking about the things I have said and written in his name. I have thought about him and about such a meeting many times. I hope he will not find fault with my work. I believe, in fact, that he will be pleased.

# FOREWORD

Almost thirty years ago, I first heard Ted Gibbons tell the story of the martyrdom with the voice of Willard Richards. His description of the martyrdom took me to Carthage and allowed me to live the last moments with the Prophet Joseph Smith. I have since that time heard Brother Gibbons relive the martyrdom many, many times. Though he has reenacted the events leading to Carthage hundreds of times, each is fresh; each is new, and each is charged with the emotion of Joseph's last great sacrifice. Perhaps this is Brother Gibbons' gift. Without question, the Lord has allowed him the blessing of testifying over and over again of the man who did more for the salvation of the human race than any other person who ever lived except the Savior.

Ted has never failed to touch me deeply with the eloquence of his presentation. The men and women who knew Joseph Smith personally surely loved him with great fervency. I feel this love flowing from Ted as he becomes, for a little while, Willard Richards himself. I doubt Willard could have loved Joseph more than Ted loves him. My own love for Joseph Smith increases under the sound of his voice, strengthened by the conviction portrayed as Ted strikes the chords of my soul.

Since the first glimpse into the past more than twenty-five years ago, I have had the opportunity of visiting Carthage and pondering there the events that transpired on a warm June afternoon. As I walked through the rooms of the jail, I could not help but hear the voice of Brother Gibbons testifying as Willard Richards. But the feelings I experienced there were no more powerful than the many times I had been taken to Carthage in spirit as I listened to a close friend testifying of the Prophet he so respects and honors.

I add my own witness to the many that have been spoken over the decades since Carthage. Joseph Smith was a true and living prophet. My life has been profoundly changed because of his searching mind and his deep devotion to the Lord Jesus Christ. I sense in a very real way that the sacrifice and suffering that culminated at Carthage were done that I might live life more fully. May all of our testimonies, combined with this testimony of Willard Richards and the many early saints, spread throughout the world, until "millions shall know Brother Joseph again."

—S. Michael Wilcox

*1*

This is a story that needs to be told, and I am the one who must tell it. In fact, I believe I was preserved to tell it for two reasons; first, because I was there, an eyewitness to virtually every event that transpired during the final weeks of the Prophet Joseph Smith's life; second, because I was one of the best friends he ever had.[1] I have his word on that. In June of 1842, two years before we came to Carthage, Joseph answered a letter from my wife.[2] He wrote to thank her for her sacrifices in his behalf. Our home was in Ramus but I spent most of my time in Nauvoo. He said to her, "I never had a greater intimacy with any man than with your husband."[3] It is from the daily reality and depth of that intimacy that I mean to tell this story. It is a love story, for as God is my witness, I loved the Prophet Joseph Smith.

Willard Richards is my name, though most people called me Doctor. In 1835 I was practicing medicine near Boston—mostly selling medicines. A cousin placed a copy of the Book of Mormon in my hands and I opened it by chance to what is now Second Nephi, chapter 2, verse 25, and read this verse:

"Adam fell that men might be; and men are that they might have joy."

Never did any verse of scripture come with greater power into my heart than that verse did. It was the most powerful scriptural text I had ever encountered. I was born to stern Presbyterian parents, and had been taught from the cradle that because of the Fall of Adam, all but the very elect of mankind were by nature irrevocably doomed to suffer the wrath of God and his angels in the eternities. And I was not one of the elect. My minister told me that a hundred times when I was a teenager. Mine was a very austere religious upbringing, with little space for joy. I had been taught to believe in a God who was too far away to hear my loudest cry for help, but close enough to take me by the scruff of the neck and drop me into the hottest corner of hell for the least infraction.

I turned to my cousin and said, "God or the devil has a hand in that book, for man never wrote it." I determined to find out which.

I borrowed the book, took it home, and began to read. Once I had commenced, I could not stop. I read the book through twice in ten days.[4] I then saw my duty clearly. I packed my bags and sold my medicines. I had learned something: God had more important things for me to do than peddle pills.[5]

I immediately began making preparations to visit Kirtland, Ohio, 750 miles west, to give the work a thorough examination. I arrived in Kirtland in October of 1836.[6] Once there, I gave the work an intense and untiring investigation until I knew for myself about its truthfulness. We cut a hole in the ice of the Chagrin River, and I was baptized by my cousin, Brigham Young, on the last day of December, 1836. I knelt, dripping, at the edge of the icy water and received the gift of the Holy Ghost. I was warmer than I had ever been in my life. I knew I had come home.

Sixty-five days later, I was ordained an Elder in the Church and was called to accompany Brigham Young on a special business mission to the Eastern states.[7] I spent three months there and returned to Kirtland on June 11. That same day I received word that Hyrum Smith wanted to see me. Joseph was very ill at that time. The next day I went to visit Hyrum and he said to me, "Willard, the prophecy has been fulfilled. Kneel down."

I knew the prophecy of which he spoke. A few months earlier Joseph had told me that I would be a part of the Church's first mission across the Atlantic to the British Isles.

I was set apart by Hyrum Smith to accompany Heber C. Kimball, Orson Hyde, and Joseph Fielding on the Church's first mission to England.[8]

While there, I had the experience of watching a modern miracle…I saw thousands of people flock to the gospel standard as the banner of the Restoration, this *ensign to the nations,* was unfurled over that great land. I had the opportunity hundreds, perhaps thousands of times, to bear my testimony of the modern day ministrations of the Lord Jesus Christ and of his Prophet, Joseph Smith, and to both see and feel the Spirit bear witness with me.

In addition to the missionary work, two other significant things happened to me in England. First, I met my wife. Now I did not go to England looking for a wife. I was at the time a 33-year-old bachelor with no intention of getting married then, nor in the foreseeable future, and especially not while I was serving as a missionary. But it was not my fault…it was Heber C. Kimball's fault. After he performed the very first baptisms in England, he sent me a note. It said, "Willard, I baptized your wife today." What was this? I knew that Heber was prophetic, but about matters as personal as this? Perhaps he might know who I was to marry, but certainly not before I knew.

When next I met him, I said, "I'd like to meet her." He thought that was a good idea, and he introduced me to a lovely young lady by the name of Jennetta Richards, the first person confirmed a member of the Church in England. She was not a relative, although we shared the same last name. When I learned her name, I suspected that Heber was having some fun with me because of our shared surnames. Heber had often taunted me about my unmarried status.

Later I went by her house to visit. I wanted to ask her father, who was a minister of the Church of England, for permission to use his church for some meetings. Perhaps that was an excuse to see her. I found out very quickly that her father was not interested in helping us in any way. However, I found out almost as quickly that I was interested in his daughter.

That was a problem. I had come to England to be a missionary, and I meant to be a good one, undistracted by other matters. But what I was feeling seemed to have a spiritual dimension to it. I felt certain that it went beyond romance. So I talked to the Lord about it and to my fellow missionaries. Finally, having received permission from Heaven and from my brethren, in my own broken way, I proposed to Jennetta. That was March 10, 1838. We were walking home from a church meeting when I discovered a small, white flower—a snowdrop. I picked it and handed it to her as I remarked: "Richards is a good name—I never want to change it. Do you, Jennetta?"

"No, I do not," was her reply, "and I think I never shall?"[9]

I expected to be released from my mission soon. Others who had come with me were already home. But a year and a half later, I was still serving. Therefore, we were married in England on September 24, 1839.[10]

The second remarkable thing that happened while I was on my mission became the foundation for these present observations. It occurred in April of 1840, but really began in July, 1838, when Joseph Smith received a revelation that mentioned me.

> Let my servant John Taylor, and also my servant John E. Page, and also my servant Wilford Woodruff, and also my servant Willard Richards, be appointed to fill the

> places of those who have fallen, and be offi-
> cially notified of their appointment.[11]

I had a premonition that the call was coming but kept my own counsel and waited on the Lord. When the call came, I was ordained a member of the Quorum of the Twelve Apostles under the hands of Brigham Young,[12] becoming the first and only member of that Quorum in this dispensation ever ordained in a foreign land.

_2_

I left England in April of 1841 and arrived in Nauvoo in August. I got off the riverboat at the head of Main Street and made my way south, asking directions until I found myself on the porch of the Homestead where Joseph and his family were still living. Joseph himself responded to my knock. When he saw me standing on his porch, he threw his arms around me and cried, "Welcome home, Doctor Richards." Commencing from the place where his hands touched my back, the Spirit began to burn in me and through me until it filled me from the soles of my feet to the crown of my head, infusing my heart and soul with this message: _Here stands the prophet of God._ Well, I knew it. I had been teaching it for four years in the British Isles, but I had never felt it with more power than then, in his arms on his porch in Nauvoo.

England had taught me the power of Joseph Smith's work. I now began to know the power of the man. We found in each other kindred spirits, and our souls were knit together.

In the months that followed my return, Joseph called me to many positions and responsibilities. I was Joseph's personal secretary, chief of his clerks, Church Historian, Clerk of the Municipal Court of Nauvoo, and member and Clerk of the City Council. He asked me to serve as Temple Recorder, as manager of the *Times and Seasons* and the *Nauvoo Neighbor,* and as general clerk of the Church. I was put in receipt of all tithes and assigned to record the transfer of all land deeds. Somewhat later I assumed responsibility for all bookkeeping in the Church as well as for the stereotype foundry and the engraving press. I wrote to my brother Levi that my life was "one eternal write, from morning till night, and from night till morning."[13]

On November 21, 1841 I left my office and walked to the temple where I assisted with the first baptisms and confirmations for the dead ever performed in a font built for that sacred purpose in this dispensation. I was one of two apostles who assisted in that work. I confirmed those who had been baptized as proxies for the dead. That night, Joseph wrote of me in his journal:

> I have been searching all my life to find a man after my own heart whom I could trust with my business in all things, and I have found him: Doctor Willard Richards is the man."[14]

During the following thirty-five months, I was seldom away from Joseph. I believe I came to know Joseph Smith better than any man who ever lived, except perhaps his brothers and his father. I was with Joseph day after day, week after week. I listened as people came to meet him, to ask questions, to investigate, some to mock and scorn. I watched his face, his eyes. I heard his voice hundreds of times as he bore testimony, as he described the golden plates, the angelic ministrants, and the experiences that brought to pass the restoration of the Gospel. Under the influence of the Spirit, he even spoke quietly a very few times of the Father and the Son and the sacred grove. And I came to know that he told the truth! Joseph Smith was God's prophet. I knew that then. I know that now.

The most dramatic evidence in my life of his prophetic calling occurred a year before we went to Carthage. I was writing at my desk in the office Joseph had built for me in the back of his store. I was sitting with my back to the Prophet, but I suddenly became aware that he was looking at me. I could feel his eyes. I turned as he arose and crossed the room to me. He stopped beside my desk and put his hands on my shoulders.

I arose to look at him, and for a moment I felt the force of his spirit probing me. After a long silence he said, "Willard, the time will come that balls will fly around you like hail, and you shall see your friends fall on the right and on the left, but there will not be a hole in your garment."[15]

Well, as I say, Joseph Smith was God's prophet. I saw that reality verified again and again. The last words he dictated to me for inclusion in his personal journal were these, spoken five days before his death in Carthage: "I told Stephen

Markham that if Hyrum and I were ever taken again, we should be massacred or I was not a prophet of God."[16]

By June of 1843, Hancock County was a powder keg. A conglomeration of apostates, religious bigots, political fanatics, and criminals had all united their forces against the Mormons, organizing a party they called the "anti-Mormons." They terrorized the Mormons on isolated farms and in the smaller settlements in the county, unroofing barns and houses, setting fire to livestock, shooting at livestock, and not infrequently at the livestock's owners.

These anti-Mormons also held widely attended public meetings where they passed resolutions of the most inflammatory kind, threatening to expel and exterminate the Mormons in Illinois. They accused us of every evil in the vocabulary of crime.[17]

In addition, in March of 1844, a secret combination had been organized in the midst of the Latter-day Saints. About 200 people, with Bibles raised in their right hands, had taken a solemn oath "before God and all holy angels" to give "their lives, their liberty, their influence, their all, for the destruction of Joseph Smith and his party."[18]

The leader of this group was William Law, a former Second Counselor in the First Presidency of the Church,[19] a man of whom Joseph Smith said, "All the sorrow I ever had in my family in the city of Nauvoo had arisen through the influence of William Law."[20]

In April of 1844, William Law told a citizen of Nauvoo named Jessie Price, "I put pistols in my pockets one night, and went to Joseph Smith's house, determined to blow his infernal brains out. I did not get the opportunity to shoot him, yet I am determined I will shoot him at the first opportunity. You will see blood and thunder and devastation in this place."[21]

To help fulfill his own prophecy, William Law, together with his brother Wilson, financed the purchase of a printing press at a cost of about $2,000.[22] The press would be used to publish an opposition newspaper in Nauvoo. William and Wilson were assisted by six other men: Francis and Chauncey Higbee, Robert and Charles Foster, Charles Ivins, and Sylvester Emmons. The name they selected for their periodical was *Nauvoo Expositor*.

*3*

When the *Expositor's* first and only issue came off the press on the 7th of June, the people of Nauvoo were outraged. The indignation of the whole community was so aroused that they threatened the annihilation of the paper. The prospectus of the paper promised exposure of "gross abuses exercised under the 'pretended' authorities of the Charter of the City of Nauvoo," and likewise revelation of "the insupportable oppression of the Ministerial powers in carrying out the unjust, illegal, and unconstitutional ordinances of the same."[23] And the paper itself attempted to expose such misbehavior and called for the repeal of the Nauvoo City Charter.

The paper also contained false accusations of gross immorality and unconscionable misconduct on the part of Church leaders. And not only accusations: a purported description of the way in which harmless, inoffensive female converts were tricked and seduced by the leading brethren was given with much detail on the second page of the paper.

There was a real possibility that the citizens of Nauvoo would take matters into their own hands and destroy the printing press and office of the *Expositor*. John Taylor, one of the leaders of the Church, said, "I do not believe that any other city in the United States, if the same charges had been made against the citizens, would have permitted it to remain even one day."[24]

At this juncture the City Council, feeling a common interest in the peace and quiet of the community, and fearing the worst consequences to Nauvoo if something were not done, but also aware that our enemies were only waiting for one overt act for an excuse to move against us, met to consider the matter.[25]

But it was a great difficulty to know how to proceed. I served as the recorder for the City Council and felt with the others the despair. We met on Saturday, the 8th of June and deliberated the matter for six and one-half hours, but adjourned without reaching a conclusion. We met again on Monday the 10th for seven and one-half additional hours. The only possibility not discussed was simply leaving the *Expositor* alone. Alderman Spencer knew what that would mean. "Shall they be suffered to go on, and bring a mob on us to murder our women and children and burn our beautiful city?" he asked.[26]

Councilor Phineas Richards said that he had not forgotten the transaction at Haun's Mill, and he recollected that his son George Spencer then lay in that well, without a winding-sheet, shroud or coffin. Phineas said he could not sit still when he saw the same spirit raging in this place. He considered the publication of the Expositor as murderous at heart as was David before the death of Uriah, and he was prepared to take a stand.

William Phelps expounded on the Constitution and on the laws and charter of Nauvoo, stating that the council had the power to declare the *Expositor* a nuisance. As such, the publication could be stopped.[27]

But that course of action was fraught with peril as well. Francis Higbee, one of the publishers, had promised, "The interest of this city is done the moment a hand is laid on that press. If they do it, the citizens of Nauvoo may date their downfall from that very hour. In ten days there will not be a Mormon left at Nauvoo."[28]

After the City Council had met on June 8th and 10th for a total of fourteen hours, Joseph, Nauvoo's Mayor, asked permission to address the Council members. He spoke with passion and eloquence: "No man is a stronger advocate for the liberty of speech and of the press than I," said Joseph. "Yet when this noble gift is utterly prostituted and abused, as in the present instance, it loses all claim to our respect and becomes as great an agent for evil as it can possibly be for good. And notwithstanding the apparent advantage we should give our enemies by this act, it behooves us as men to act independent of all secondary influences, to perform the part of men of enlarged minds, to boldly and fearlessly discharge the duties devolving upon us by declaring a nuisance and removing this filthy, libelous, and seditious sheet from our midst."[29]

Following this appeal, a vote was taken and a resolution passed declaring the *Nauvoo Expositor* a nuisance and instructing that it be removed. The order was delivered to Mayor Joseph Smith and he directed John P. Green, city marshal, to comply. He also alerted the Nauvoo Legion in case their assistance was needed.

Marshal Green, assisted by some members of the Nauvoo Legion, proceeded to the premises of the *Nauvoo Expositor,* forced open the door, and brought the press into the street, where it was destroyed with hammers. The type was scattered and the second edition, about half-completed, was burned.

Although they were in no personal danger, the eight publishers fled Nauvoo, some to Carthage and others to Warsaw, the two centers of anti-Mormon sentiment. Charles Foster, when he arrived in Warsaw the next day, wrote a letter to Tom Sharp, publisher and editor of the most bitter of all anti-Mormon newspapers, the *Warsaw* Signal. The letter, published on June 12, began:

> Mr. Sharp: I hasten to inform you of the UNPARALLELED OUTRAGE, perpetrated upon our rights and interests by the ruthless, lawless, ruffian band of MORMON MOBOCRATS at the dictation of the UNPRINCIPLED wretch Joe Smith. (All emphasis in original)

Thereafter followed a distorted account of the *Expositor* affair.[30]

Tom Sharp penned an editorial immediately following Foster's letter, calling the citizens to action. He wrote:

> We have only to state, that this is suffi-
> cient! War and extermination is inevitable!
> Citizens ARISE, ONE and ALL! Can you
> stand by and suffer such INFERNAL DEV-
> ILS! to rob men of their property and rights,
> without avenging them? We have no time for
> comment. Every man will make his own. Let
> it be made with POWDER and BALL![31] (All
> emphasis in original)

The day Foster's letter was written a mass meeting was held in Carthage. Francis Higbee attended that meeting in Carthage and addressed those men there assembled. He told them that he had a personal knowledge of the Mormons from their earliest history-throughout their hellish career in Missouri and this state-which has been characterized by the darkest and most diabolical deeds which have ever disgraced humanity. Why Francis made his home with such diabolical and disgraceful people for ten years, under such awful circumstances, he did not explain.

Five hundred men were at that meeting. They passed several resolutions, among them this one:

> *Resolved*, that we hold ourselves at all
> times in readiness to co-operate with our fel-

low citizens in this state, Missouri, and Iowa,
to exterminate, utterly exterminate the wicked
and abominable Mormon leaders, the authors
of our troubles.

Language in other resolutions indicated that bodies of armed men were gathering in Missouri and Iowa to assist and that cannons and ammunition were being transported from Missouri to exterminate the Mormons.[32]

Two days after the *Expositor's* press was destroyed, Constable Bettisworth arrived from Carthage with a warrant issued by Justice Morrison on complaint of Francis Higbee, for the arrest of the Mayor and the City Council of Nauvoo. The charge was riot, which was supposed to have occurred in conjunction with the destruction of the press of the *Nauvoo Expositor*.

The charge was a falsehood, and Higbee knew it, for the destruction had been handled in an orderly fashion. When Joseph received and read the warrant, he pointed out that the language on the warrant indicated that it was returnable before Justice Morrison or "some other Justice of the Peace."[33] Joseph then offered to go immediately before the nearest Justice of the Peace, but he refused to go to Carthage.

Two weeks earlier Joseph had been in Carthage with friends to answer charges of perjury and adultery. On that occasion, an apostate named Robert Foster, in a spirit of repentance and reconciliation, had warned John P. Green, the Marshall of Nauvoo: "For God's sake, don't suffer that man,

Joseph Smith, to go out of doors, for if he steps outside of the door, his blood will be spilt."[34]

Joseph had also heard about the meeting in Carthage the day before and he knew that there were people in Carthage who would kill him. Yet when the Prophet opposed going there, Bettisworth insisted, becoming irate and profane. Bettisworth was determined to carry Joseph and Hyrum to Carthage before Morrison and before no other.[35] But Joseph knew his rights. He became so indignant at this abuse of his privilege, granted by the very writ Bettisworth had carried, of going before "some other justice," that he went before the Municipal Court of Nauvoo and obtained a writ of *habeas corpus.* A hearing was held, and the judge determined that there had been no riot and that the complaint was malicious. Joseph was sent home and Higbee was ordered to pay court costs.[36]

Predictably, the outrage in Hancock County increased. Things which were already bad now became much worse. Participants at a Warsaw mass meeting echoed the resolutions of the Carthage meeting. They were ready and willing to "exterminate, utterly exterminate, the wicked and abominable Mormon leaders..."[37]

Most citizens of Hancock County, who heard only the anti-Mormon side of the *Expositor* affair, were convinced that justice had not been served in the Mormon court at Nauvoo. They were incensed. Depredations and threats against Mormons outside of Nauvoo increased dramatically.[38]

Joseph made contact with Judge Jesse B. Thomas, circuit court judge for Hancock County, and asked for counsel.[39] Judge Thomas advised him to have a trial and examination of the charges specified in the writ from Justice Morrison, but he suggested that Joseph go elsewhere in Hancock County for the trial and not have it before a Mormon in Nauvoo.[40]

Therefore, Joseph and the City Council were rearrested on the charge of riot and tried before Squire Daniel Wells, a non-Mormon. After a lengthy, detailed examination, all charges were dismissed.[41]

Things did not improve, however. They got worse. To protect the city and its inhabitants from the mobs that were organizing to plunder and destroy Nauvoo and to murder its inhabitants,[42] Joseph declared martial law. Members of the Legion from outlying areas were ordered to Nauvoo. When they arrived, the Legion stood at full strength.[43]

In addition to these precautionary measures, Joseph was in frequent contact with Illinois' Governor Ford, sending regular letters to keep him aware of the situation. Other Church leaders also wrote to Ford. But Joseph's letter of the June 16 was inscribed with a special intensity. He wrote: "I wish, urgently wish, your Excellency to come down in person and investigate the whole matter without delay, and cause peace to be restored to the country. I know not but what this will be the only means of stopping an effusion of blood."[44]

*4*

On June 21, Governor Ford arrived at Carthage and addressed a letter to "The Honorable Mayor and Common Council of the City of Nauvoo," asking them to send one or more well-informed and discreet individuals to lay before him the Mormon version of what was happening in Hancock County.[45] The council appointed me, John Taylor, and John M. Bernhisel. I did not make the trip, however, but remained behind to prepare additional documents.[46]

Elders Taylor and Bernhisel arrived at Carthage about 11:00 p.m. on June 21st. They found Carthage filled with our most bitter enemies. Elder Taylor said that before he got to the hotel, his life was threatened twice. He suspected these men might make an attempt to separate him and Dr. Bernhisel to deprive them of their documents and perhaps of their lives. He did not sleep at all that night but lay awake with his pistols under his pillow, waiting for an emergency.[47]

The next morning Governor Ford kept them waiting for an audience until after 10:00. When the meeting finally commenced, they found the governor surrounded by their enemies. William Law was there, along with his brother Wilson and the Fosters and the Higbees. Joseph H. Jackson was also there—a man who was reported to have a counterfeiting operation in Nauvoo and who had previously threatened to kidnap Hyrum Smith's daughter and shoot anyone who tried to interfere.[48]

John Taylor was disgusted. If he had been on a private errand, he would have gone home. But he was on public business and did not have a choice. He and his companion told the governor they were prepared to give him all of the pertinent information, supported by testimony and affidavit, about what had happened in Nauvoo.[49] Taylor and Bernheisel attempted to do this, but found it impossible. During their conversations with the governor, they were frequently, rudely, and impudently contradicted by the anti-Mormons. When the governor opened and read out loud a number of Taylor's documents, the crowd exposed the true nature of their souls, calling out, "That's a lie!" "That's a damned lie!" and "That's an infernal falsehood!"[50]

Taylor and Bernhisel explained to the governor that they had fulfilled the law, both in letter and intent. Ford was not satisfied. Neither were those that were with him. Ford (a politician, after all), seemed determined that those around him be appeased. After pledging his faith that those named in the warrant would be guaranteed perfect safety,[51] Ford asked the two brethren to remain while he prepared a written communication for Joseph Smith. Governor Ford kept them waiting about five hours for this instrument.

When they returned to Nauvoo the night of June 22, Elders Taylor and Bernhisel met with Joseph in the Mansion House and delivered the letter from Governor Ford.

Joseph read the letter quietly to himself, then out loud to all of us. In it, Ford insisted that, notwithstanding the former trials, those named in the warrant should submit to arrest "by the same constable, by virtue of the same warrant, and be tried before the same magistrate whose authority had heretofore been resisted." This from a man who, in the week before the martyrdom, promised the Mormons protection and a fair trail at least six times.

> "You know the excitement of the public mind, do not tempt it too far. A very little matter may do a very great injury; and if you are disposed to continue the causes of excitement and render a force necessary to coerce submission, I would say that your city was built, as it were, upon a keg of powder which a very little spark may explode. And I will also guarantee the safety of all such persons as may thus be brought to this place from Nauvoo, either for trial or as witnesses for the accused."
>
> "Nothing short of this," wrote Ford, "can vindicate the dignity of violated law and allay the just excitement of the people."[52]

In spite of the governor's guarantee of safety for all persons who should come to Carthage, Joseph was troubled. He folded the letter, laid it on the table, then paced the floor for a moment. I could see that he was upset. It puzzled me. "Joseph, what can be the matter?" I asked him, "The governor has promised you protection and a fair trial."

He looked at me as though he were surprised that I did not understand. "Willard," he finally said, "I want you to write something for my journal."

I sat at his desk and wrote these words as he dictated them to me They are the last words Joseph asked to have included in his journal. With this statement, his personal history ends. He said, "I told Stephen Markham that if Hyrum and I were ever taken again, we should be massacred, or I was not a prophet of God." When I finished writing, Joseph turned to his brother.

"There is no mercy...no mercy here," he said.

Hyrum agreed. "No, just as surely as we fall into their hands we are dead men."

"Yes. What shall we do, Brother Hyrum?"

"I don't know."

Later, however, Joseph did know. The light of revelation flashed in his eyes.

"It is clear to my mind what we must do," he said. "All they want is Hyrum and myself. Tell the people to go on about their business and not to collect in groups, but to scatter about. There is no doubt they will come here and search for us. Let them search. They will not harm you in person or in property, not even a hair of your heads. We will cross the river tonight and go away to the west."

On several occasions, Joseph had prophesied that the Saints would become a mighty people in the midst of the Rocky Mountains. It was to this location that Joseph intended to flee.[53]

Joseph, Hyrum, and I got Porter Rockwell out of bed. We spent about two hours locating a boat. Porter then rowed us across the river to Montrose, Iowa. The skiff was so leaky that we kept busy bailing with our boots and shoes to keep it from sinking. When we arrived at the opposite bank, we went to the home of William Jordan, arriving there about 5:00 in the morning. Porter was sent back across the river to obtain horses for the trip west. We told Porter to return that night, now June 23, under cover of darkness so no one would know of our location.[54]

Porter returned during the afternoon. He did not bring horses, but he brought Brothers Reynolds Cahoon, Lorenzo Wasson, and Hiram Kimball. They found us in a small room in a house belonging to William Jordan, packing our provisions. Brother Cahoon delivered a letter from Joseph's wife, Emma, and reported that there had been a posse in Nauvoo that morning.

They spent three hours looking for Joseph and Hyrum. One of the posse had indicated that it was Governor Ford's intention to send troops to Nauvoo who would, if necessary, remain for three years until Joseph and Hyrum were in custody.[55] The posse had been to the Mansion House, of course, and had made some threats that had caused Emma great alarm.[56] They had presented Emma with another letter from the governor, who again promised protection and a fair trial. But Emma had been told that her husband was gone to the Rockies. Later that morning, however, when she found Rockwell in town and learned that her husband had not yet departed she sent a verbal plea and a letter with Porter for Joseph to return and stand trial in Carthage. It is impossible to criticize Emma for her actions in this matter. She had lost six children at childbirth or shortly thereafter, including one adopted baby. Now she had a baby due in only a few months and she wanted Joseph close at hand. In addition she had the governor's promise of protection. But it was not just Emma who was concerned. Many of the Church members were sorely tried to think their prophet would abandon them in this moment of crisis.[57]

Even so, Joseph had no plans to return. He knew what would happen if he went to Carthage. Joseph did not want to he a martyr. He did not want to seal his testimony with his blood. He wanted to be a father and a prophet and a teacher. So he was not going to give himself up, even after Cahoon informed him that the governor, for the third time, had pledged his faith, and the faith of the state, to protect him.[58]

Then these three brethren did an awful thing. They accused Joseph of cowardice for wishing to leave his people. It was, they said, like the fable in which, when the wolves came, the shepherd fled and left the sheep to be devoured.[59]

This was a tragic blindness on the part of these brethren. They had wounded the Prophet in a place where he was wholly vulnerable—his love for his people. Joseph stood for a moment, quietly, thoughtfully. I think he knew then that he would never see the Rocky Mountains. A year and a half earlier in a public sermon he had said, "I shall not be sacrificed until my time comes; then I shall he offered freely."[60] A few months later, he said it even more explicitly: "...I prophesy they never will have power to kill me till my work is accomplished and I am ready to die."[61] In the previous months he had declared many additional times that he would one day give his life for the kingdom. Perhaps he saw in the accusations of these supposed brethren that his time had come. Finally he raised his head and searched the eyes of these men.

"If my life is of no value to my friends, it is of none to myself," he said. Joseph then turned to Porter Rockwell and said, "Port, what shall I do?"

Porter replied, "You are the oldest and ought to know best. As you make your bed, I will lie with you."

Joseph then turned to Hyrum and said, "Brother Hyrum, you are the oldest. What shall we do?"

Hyrum said, "Let us go back and give ourselves up and see the thing out."

Once again Joseph wrapped himself in his thoughts, looking for another way and finding none. "If you go back, I shall go with you," he said, "but we shall be butchered."

"No, no," Hyrum replied. "Let's go back and put our trust in God…the Lord is in it. If we live, or have to die, we will be reconciled to our fate."[62]

The decision was made. Joseph requested a boat for 5:30 p.m. and then dictated a letter to Governor Ford in which he said, "I now offer to come to Carthage on the morrow, as early as shall be convenient for your posse to escort us into head-quarters, provided we can have a fair trial, not be abused, and have all things done in due form of law, without partiality. You can depend on my honor without the show of a great armed force to produce excitement in the minds of the timid."[63]

From the Mansion House the night before, Joseph had written Governor Ford detailing his fears about the very thing he was now determined to do.

"We dare not come," he had declared. "Writs, we are assured, are issued against us in various parts of the country. For what? To drag us from place to place, from court to court, across the creeks and prairies, till some bloodthirsty villain could find his opportunity to shoot us. We dare not come, though your Excellency promises protection."[64]

Now, having written this more recent letter, Joseph would go to Carthage. Seeing his determination, some of those who had induced him to return would now have interposed, but Joseph stood firm.[65] From this moment on, he would comply with every demand of the governor. As they walked to the river, Joseph delayed and fell behind the others, speaking with Rockwell. Someone shouted for him to hurry to the boat.

"It is of no use to hurry," he said, "for we are going back to he slaughtered."[66]

# 5

We started across the river about 5:30 that evening. When we had disembarked at the bottom of Parley Street, Joseph expressed a desire to speak to the people. Porter offered to get them out by starlight to hear him, but when Joseph got home and saw his family, he decided to spend the night with them instead.[67]

During the night, Theodore Turley and Jedediah Grant rode to Carthage with Joseph's letter, then returned with the governor's response. They did not arrive in Nauvoo until 4:00 a.m.

They reported that the governor had demanded that General Smith and his party should be in Carthage by 10:00 the next morning with those named in the writ, and that they should come without an armed escort. If Joseph did not comply, Governor Ford warned that the city of Nauvoo would be destroyed along with all the men, women, and children that were in it.[68]

Elders Turley and Grant tried to warn Joseph of the excitement and danger evident in Carthage, but Joseph would not hear a word. He was determined to go to Carthage and give himself up to the governor. Joseph issued instructions to gather horses for the journey.[69]

Hundreds gathered at the Mansion House the next morning to see the brethren depart. In the early morning light they seemed filled with a solemn apprehension of forthcoming danger. Many implored the Prophet to change his mind. His small sons were clinging to his clothing, with Emma weeping by his side.

Finally Joseph's mother, Lucy, expressed the fear they all felt.

"My son, my son," she said, "can you leave me without promising to return? Some forty times I have seen you from me dragged, but never before without saying you would return. What say you now, my son?"

Joseph raised his hand for silence and spoke to those assembled.

"My friends, my brethren, I love you," he said. "I love the city of Nauvoo too well to save my life at your expense. If I go not to them, they will come here and act out the horrid Missouri scenes in Nauvoo. I may prevent it. I fear not death; my work is done. Keep the faith and I will die for Nauvoo."[70]

From the Mansion House the men named in the writ, together with several friends, rode to the temple. Joseph looked solemnly at this monument to his inspiration and industry, then turned and gazed over the city, emotion filling him and spilling out of him. He looked at the beautiful blue sweep of the Mississippi, at the white frame and red brick homes. When he could control his feelings, he spoke, saying:

"This is the loveliest place and the best people under the heavens. Little do they know the trials that await them ."[71]

At the outskirts of the city, the riders stopped at the home of a friend named Squire Daniel Wells, who was confined to his sickbed. After Joseph visited with him, he took his leave, saying, "Squire Wells, I wish you to cherish my memory, and not think me the worst man in the world either."[72]

At ten minutes to 10:00 we arrived at the Fellows' farmhouse, four miles west of Carthage, where we stopped to rest the horses and take refreshment. While there, we met Captain Dunn with a troop of about sixty mounted militia coming from Carthage. Captain Dunn presented Joseph with an order from the governor demanding that the Nauvoo Legion surrender their state-owned arms.

This seemed to be madness. Were the Mormons in Nauvoo to be left unarmed and defenseless, with armed mobs only miles away in both Warsaw and Carthage vowing to seek their destruction and extermination? Our minds returned to Missouri, where Mormons were disarmed, but not the mobs. To our amazement, Joseph, who was the commanding General of the Nauvoo Legion, promptly countersigned the order.[73]

Joseph then came across the yard to where we were standing. "I am going like a lamb to the slaughter," he said, "but I am calm as a summer's morning. I have a conscience void of offense toward God and toward all men. I shall die innocent, and it shall yet he said of me, 'He was murdered in cold blood.'"[74]

Captain Dunn was rightly concerned that the members of the Nauvoo Legion, circumstances being what they were, might not willingly surrender their weapons. He asked Joseph and his party to accompany him hack to Nauvoo to facilitate the transfer and collection of arms. Joseph agreed and sent word to the governor explaining the delay. We then returned to Nauvoo.

Joseph sent a message to Major General Dunham with instructions for members of the Legion to deposit their individual arms at the Masonic Lodge on Main Street. Members of the Legion were reluctant to give up their weapons, fearing a repetition of the Missouri massacre, but they did as the Prophet requested.[75] In fact, only about three hundred legionaries had state weapons, and many of them had their own as well. Thus the fire power of the Legion was not greatly reduced.

While in Nauvoo, Joseph twice visited his house to bid his family farewell. He was subdued and thoughtful, stating repeatedly that he expected to be murdered.[76] Joseph was also apprehensive about his sons, asking Emma three times before he left if she would train his sons to walk in the faith of their father.[77] Before leaving his home for the final time, Joseph spoke of the child Emma was expecting. "If this baby is a boy," he told her, "I wish you to name him David Hyrum, for I have always loved that name." The baby was born on the 17th of November, 1844, and given the name Joseph had requested.

Back at the Masonic lodge, where the weapons were being collected, the Prophet took one of John Fremont's maps of the West and spoke to some members of the Nauvoo Legion, "Now I will show you the travels of this people." He traced a course across Iowa to the Missouri River, and then on to the Great Basin and the Rocky Mountains. He pointed to a spot and said, "Here you will come to the Great Salt Lake valley."

When those close by asked where he would be at that time, Joseph said, "I shall never go there."[78]

By 6:00 p.m. the arms were collected and the party was ready for the return to Carthage. As they rode away from the Masonic lodge, Joseph spoke to the few Legionnaires still standing about. "Boys, if I don't come back, take care of yourselves," he said, "I am going like a lamb to the slaughter."[79]

When we passed the Prophet's farm on the road to Carthage, about two miles from Nauvoo. Joseph looked at it longingly. After we had passed, he turned around several times to look again. Some of the company were concerned about the lateness of the hour and the need to get to Carthage. Some men even made remarks about needless delays, which caused Joseph to turn and say, "If some of you had got such a farm, and knew that you would never see it again, would you not want to take a good look at it for the last time?"[80]

After these words, Joseph turned and rode off to Carthage to turn himself over to his enemies.

*6*

We arrived in Carthage just before midnight, making our way toward the Hamilton House for a night's lodging. We found eleven or twelve hundred Illinois state troops quartered on the public square, ordered to active duty from surrounding communities by the governor of the state. Many of them, especially the Carthage Greys, were aroused by our passage.

"Where is the damned prophet?" they shouted. "Stand away, boys, and let us shoot the damned Mormons! Clear the way and let us have a view of the Mormon prophet. He's seen the last of Nauvoo! We'll use him up now and kill every damned Mormon on the river!"[81]

The Carthage Greys followed us to the hotel, whooping, yelling, and hooting like savages.[82] The noise aroused Governor Ford, who put his head out of the window.

"Gentlemen, gentlemen! I know your great anxiety to see Mr. Smith, which is natural enough. But it is quite too late tonight for you to have that opportunity. I assure you, gentlemen, that you shall have that privilege tomorrow morning, as I will cause him to pass before the troops upon the square. And now I wish you, with this assurance, quietly and peacefully to withdraw to your quarters."[83] To this there was a faint "Hurrah for Tom Ford!" and the crowd dispersed. As we retired for the night, Joseph had a question for me. "Willard, did you have a happy fortieth birthday?" I told him I thought I could remember some that were happier.

Early the next morning, Joseph, Hyrum, and those named in the original warrant issued on the charge of riot voluntarily surrendered themselves to Constable Bettisworth. They were then re-arrested on the original warrant (for the third time), so that they could stand trial before the issuing magistrate, Justice Morrison, to "vindicate the dignity of violated law, and allay the just excitement of the people."[84]

Immediately afterwards, Joseph and Hyrum were arrested again, this time on a charge of treason against the state and people of Illinois, for declaring martial law in Nauvoo.[85]

By 8:30 that morning, the 1,200 to 1,300 troops in Carthage were in formation in the public square.[86]

At 9:15, the governor came to our room and requested that Joseph and Hyrum walk with him through the troops. So Joseph, Hyrum, and I accompanied the governor and Brigadier General Deming, who commanded all the militia in Carthage, to the general's headquarters. All was quiet until a company of the Carthage Greys flocked around the headquarters' doors, making an uproar over the apparent extension of a military courtesy to the Smiths.[87]

At seven minutes to 10:00, we arrived before the assembled troops and commenced to pass in review. Joseph and

Hyrum were introduced some twenty times as Generals Joseph and Hyrum Smith, their rank in the Nauvoo Legion.

All went well until the Prophet and his brother were introduced to the Carthage Greys, who refused to receive them by their military titles. Some of the officers threw their hats in the air and drew their swords, saying they would introduce themselves to the "damned Mormons" in a different style.

The governor tried to calm the troops, but found it difficult. He brought a table from the General's tent, ascended, and made a speech lasting nearly quarter of an hour. He concluded by promising the troops there assembled "full satisfaction," whatever that is supposed to mean to men screaming for blood.

The Greys should have been pacified by the governor's address. He was an excellent orator. But they continued to behave in such an uproarious fashion that General Deming placed them under arrest. They were later released without punishment after the governor petitioned the general in their behalf.[88]

Joseph retained attorneys H. T. Reid and James Woods to represent him. The next day, Woods said he believed the governor had made a near-fatal mistake in offering to introduce the Smiths to the assembled Carthage troops, Ford being fully aware of their hostility. Woods also indicated that he was told there were more than a hundred loaded guns present on the public square for shooting Joseph Smith, but because the lawyer had walked on Joseph's right, between him and the troops, the troops had refrained from the attempt.[89]

That afternoon, several of the officers of the militia and other gentlemen curious to see and question the Prophet visited him at the hotel. After a brief discussion, Joseph asked his own question: "Gentlemen, I wish you to answer me honestly," he said. "Do I appear to be the sort of desperate character that my enemies have represented me to be?"

After a prolonged and uncomfortable silence, one man offered a reply: "No, sir. Your appearance would indicate the very contrary, General Smith. But we cannot see into your heart; neither can we tell what are your intentions."

"That is very true, gentlemen," Joseph replied. "You cannot see what is in my heart. But I can see what is in your hearts, and I will tell you what I see. I can see that you thirst for blood, and that nothing but my blood will satisfy you. And inasmuch as you and this people thirst for blood, I prophesy in the name of the Lord that you will witness scenes of blood and sorrow to your entire satisfaction. Your souls shall be perfectly satiated with blood, and many of you shall have the opportunity to face the cannon's mouth from sources that you think not of.[90] And those people that desire this great evil upon me and my brethren shall be filled with regret and sorrow because of the scenes of desolation and distress that await them. They shall seek for peace and shall not be able to find it. Gentlemen, you will find what I have told you to be true."

In this case, as in every other, the vision of the Joseph Smith was clear and precise, for men from this area of Illinois suffered greatly in the Civil War. But they were to face other unexpected disasters as well. On the 23rd of February, 1847, the 1st and 2nd Illinois regiments, along with other troops from Kentucky, were nearly annihilated in the war with Mexico during the Battle of Buena Vista. In a slaughter that lasted only twenty minutes, nearly all of the Illinoisans, among whom must have been some who listened to Joseph Smith's prediction, were cut down in a perfect satiation of blood. Gregg wrote of this event,

> The whole gorge, from the plateau to its mouth, was strewed with our dead. All dead! No wounded there—not a man; for the infantry had rushed down the sides and completed the work with the bayonet.[91]

At about 4:00 p.m. on June 25th, Joseph, Hyrum, and thirteen members of the Nauvoo City Council were taken to court. To their amazement they found the man presiding there was not Justice Morrison, about whom the governor had made such a fuss, but Robert Smith, a Justice of the Peace. Smith was also captain of the Carthage Greys who had previously been arrested for mutiny.[92] As soon as we entered the courtroom, Chauncey Highee, working with the prosecution, called for an adjournment. Lawyers Reid and Woods objected, of course. Adjournment meant bail would be set, and it was contrary to law to set bail or require recognizance unless the defendants acknowledged their guilt or there were witnesses to prove the charges. However, it being freely admitted that the *Expositor's* press had been destroyed and that the courts had jurisdiction to hear any case, the defendants agreed to bail to prevent, if possible, any increase in excitement among the people.

If convicted for the crime of riot, the guilty could have been fined no more than $200 under Illinois state law. Yet the magistrate, in an attempt to exceed the brethren's resources and thereby imprison them, set bail at $500 per man—a total of $7,500. But we raised enough to cover even this excessive amount. Because so many friends of the Prophet and his brother gave cash or security for everything they had, the prisoners were all released.[93] Justice Smith adjourned the proceedings without calling the treason case.[94]

Many of the members of the City Council departed immediately for Nauvoo, but Joseph and Hyrum, with a few friends, remained in Carthage for a promised interview with the governor. Not long after the court adjourned, we were intercepted by Constable Bettisworth as we left the Hamilton House dining room. He insisted we go to prison at once.

Of course Joseph refused to go. He was free on bail. The constable knew that. He had been in the courtroom during the proceedings. When he continued to insist on their incarceration, Joseph declared, "Constable, what can be the matter with you? As you well know, Sir, we are free on bail, and cannot be taken into custody without an order from the court!"

The constable claimed to have such an order and Joseph demanded to see a copy of the mittimnus, the judicial order committing us to jail. Bettisworth refused to present one, whereupon Joseph's lawyers stated that the prisoners were entitled to be brought before the Justice of the Peace for examination before they could be taken to jail. To our surprise, the constable then produced a mittimus, signed by our enemy Robert Smith, indicating that Joseph and Hyrum had been arrested on a charge of *treason*. It said they had been brought before him, Robert Smith, for a hearing on that charge, but that the trial had been postponed due to lack of material witnesses. Joseph and Hyrum were therefore to he taken to jail and held there until discharged by due course of law.[95]

The recitals of this mittimus were wholly untrue. Joseph and Hyrum had been arrested on a charge of treason, but not so much as one word about that charge had been spoken in the presence of Justice Smith. And no law in Illinois permitted a justice to commit persons to jail without examining the probability of their guilt.[96]

Joseph and Hyrum were furious with these bold-faced, illegal proceedings, but the constable insisted they go to jail. Lawyer Woods went for the governor, and together they confronted Justice Smith, who explained that he had issued the warrant of committal because the prisoners were not safe at the hotel.[97]

Elder John Taylor also sought out the governor. He informed Ford of the characters of those who had made the oaths against Hyrum and the Prophet. He explained that the actions of the justice were totally vexatious, and the charges absolutely false. He also informed the governor of the illegality of any incarceration without a hearing. Although the governor expressed sorrow with the proceedings, he indicated that he felt it was best to let the law take its course.[98]

As I recorded these events, I was outraged. I envisioned Governor Ford in the place of Pilate, standing before the Sanhedrin of Captain Smith and his Carthage Greys, washing his hands. Elder Taylor expressed similar feelings to the governor, but Ford simply repeated his promise of protection, and promised a careful judicial review and examination of the charges without mistreatment or ridicule of the parties involved.

"If we are to be subject to mob rule," said Elder Taylor to Governor Ford, "and to be dragged contrary to law into prison at the insistence of every scoundrel whose oaths can be bought for a dram of whiskey, your protection avails very little, and we have miscalculated your promises."[99]

Elder Taylor and others feared a plan existed to murder the prisoners on their way to the jail. Captain Dunn, who on the road to Carthage had promised that Joseph should be protected, even if it were at the expense of his own life,[100] now arrived at the Hamilton House. His twenty soldiers accompanied Joseph and his companions to the jail.[101]

But additional protection was needed. Stephen Markham was one of Joseph's bodyguards. He was fond of saying that he had no idea what fear was for he had never experienced it. He is reported to have said on occasion, "When God made me, he left that part out." Markham had a large hickory walking stick which he had carved himself and to which he had given a name: he called it his "rascal-beater."

Dan Jones* had become a member of the church the year before (1843). He knew and loved the Prophet and he had a smaller walking stick of his own. The two men walked on either side of Joseph and Hyrum, keeping off the drunken rabble who several times broke through the soldiers' ranks.[102]

* In the early 1850's, George A. Smith, who had become Church Historian at the death of Willard Richards, asked several men who had been witnesses to the events of the martyrdom to give him their recollections. Among those who responded was Dan Jones, who provided a dramatic but somewhat flowery 26-page account. Many of his insights are unique. Therefore, the portion of his account dealing directly with the martyrdom is included as an appendix to this work.

# 7

The prisoners and friends were received by jailer George Stigall, and put in the criminal's cell on the second floor. It was a filthy, vermin-infested place, unbearably vile. I honestly think the cell had not been cleaned since the jail was completed in 1839. We begged the jailer to give us something less polluted and he finally moved us to the slightly more spacious and much cleaner debtor's apartment on the floor below. We conversed until about 11:30, offered prayer, and then, because there was no furniture of any kind in the room, slept stretched out on the floor until about 6:00 the morning of the 26th.[103]

After we had eaten breakfast with the jailer, he suggested that we move upstairs to his bedroom, located on the southeast corner of the second floor. We were very much gratified by these new accommodations. As we examined the room, we discovered the door to be of half-inch common panel, and so badly warped that it would not latch. The door had no lock of any description, of course. It was a bedroom door. Dan Jones and Stephen Markham spent most of the forenoon working on the door with a penknife to get it on the latch, preparing to fortify the room in case of attack.[104]

At 9:27 the governor arrived for the interview he had promised Joseph the day before. Governor Ford insisted they discuss the difficulties associated with the *Expositor* and the refusal of the persons named in the writ to be accountable in Carthage before the issuing magistrate. Joseph explained his position, as well as the outrage the *Expositor* had caused in the hearts of the citizens of Nauvoo.

There is not," said Joseph, "another city in the United States that would have suffered such an indignity for twenty-four hours."[105]

After further review of the matter, and after insisting that the City Council had acted in its best judgment, Joseph said, "The thing, after all, is only a legal difficulty. The courts, I should judge, are competent to decide on this matter. If our act was illegal, we are willing to meet it."[106]

For Joseph, the abatement of the *Expositor* was not really the issue.

"When you, sir, required us to come out here," he said, "we came, not because it was legal, but because you required it of us.[107] There is no law in Illinois nor on earth that could have compelled us to come here and be tried for the third time on the same warrant."

Joseph had already explained the facts relating to Constable Bettisworth's illegal demand that Joseph be tried in Carthage and in no other place, when the writ upon which he was arrested provided him the option of going before some other justice on the beach in Hancock County.

Joseph spoke of the writ of *habeas corpus* issued by the municipal court, and of the investigation that followed. He told the governor of Judge Thomas' counsel to go before a non-Mormon outside of Nauvoo to have an impartial examination of the facts.

"We went before Squire Wells, with whom you are well acquainted," said Joseph. "Both parties were present. Witnesses were called on both sides. The case was fully investigated, and we were dismissed."[108]

What Joseph said was true. Joseph was in Carthage not because the law required it of him but because the governor had requested it of him. He told the governor that he had expected better treatment than to be thrown into jail.

"And now, having fulfilled my part, sir, as an American citizen," concluded Joseph, "I call upon you, Governor Ford, to deliver us from this place and rescue us from this outrage."[109]

More questions were asked, with much discussion, and the interview lasted above three quarters of an hour. But the best the governor would offer was to say, "Concerning your being in jail, I am sorry for that. I wish it had been otherwise. I hope you will soon be released, but I cannot interfere.

When the governor indicated that he was planning a trip to Nauvoo, Joseph said, "If you go, sir, I wish to go along. I refuse not to answer to any law, but I do not consider myself safe here."

"I do not know that I shall go tomorrow to Nauvoo," said the governor, "but if I do, I will take you along."[111] Both Taylor and I wrote it as he said it.

Governor Ford left the jail about 10:15, knowing that Joseph's concern about being left in Carthage was well-founded. He had listened to the mortal threats of the Greys on three different occasions. The Laws, the Higbees, and Robert Foster had publicly avowed that "there was nothing against these men. The law could not reach them, but powder and ball would, and they should not go out of Carthage alive."[112]

The editor of the *Alton Telegraph*, a local newspaper, described the atmosphere in Carthage this way: "No one (not even the governor) could close his ears against the murmurs that ran throughout the entire community. Little squads could he seen at the taverns, at the tents of the soldiers, and in every part of town…Expressions falling from the lips of numbers there assembled could leave no other impression upon any sane mind than that they were determined the Smiths should not escape summary punishment."[113]

Joseph was more distraught than I had ever seen him. We tried to cheer him up, but he remarked, "I've had a good deal of anxiety about my safety since I left Nauvoo, which I've never had before when under arrest. I cannot help these feelings, and they have depressed me."[114]

Joseph and Hyrum preached to the guards from the windows. Several guards were relieved before their time because they were convinced of the prisoners' innocence. One said,

"Let's go home, boys, for I will not fight any longer against these men."[115]

I spent the early part of the afternoon writing at the Prophet's dictation. John Taylor sang to offer some entertainment.

At about 2:30, Constable Bettisworth came to the jail with an order to the jailer from Justice Smith demanding that he surrender his prisoners.[116] Stigall knew of no law authorizing him to deliver up to a Justice of the Peace prisoners committed to his keeping "until discharged by due course of law," and he refused to give them up.[117]

But Robert Smith was determined to give some semblance of legality to his incarceration of the Smiths, and as captain of the Carthage Greys he knew how to overcome the jailer's reluctance. The constable returned an hour later with a company of Carthage Greys. They compelled Stigall, against his will and conviction of duty, to deliver Joseph and Hyrum.

In addition, a mob whose appearance was increasingly ominous gathered around the jail. Realizing it was useless to resist, Joseph put on his hat, descended the stairs to the street, and linked arms with Hyrum and the worst mobocrat he could find. With a guard close at hand, I followed them to the courtroom.[118]

Lawyer Woods was indignant and objected enthusiatically to the entire affair. Not only were the prisoners illegally committed, but once they were committed, the magistrate had no further power over them. But as this was the same magistrate who had imprisoned Joseph and then, as captain of the Greys, had forced him from jail, Woods' arguments availed little.[119]

Justice Smith insisted that a hearing on the charge of treason be held at once. But all those who might have spoken for Joseph and Hyrum had returned to Nauvoo, so Woods asked for a continuance until the next day. By 5:30 we were back in jail. Shortly after our return, John Smith, Joseph and Hyrum's uncle, visited us. He asked if Joseph could again escape his enemies. Joseph replied, "My brother Hyrum thinks I shall." Throughout all these proceedings, Hyrum remained optimistic.[120] This was not a sentiment shared by his brother.

Throughout that evening, the troops stationed in Carthage urged the governor on to Nauvoo. They insisted on searching for bogus money allegedly minted in the Mormon city.[121] Now that the Nauvoo Legion was disarmed, they were particularly eager for a march on the Mormon stronghold. For days their women had prepared supplies for an eventual siege.[122] To this end, 400 to 500 Warsaw troops were ordered by General Demming to Golden's Point, a few miles short of Nauvoo.[123] Governor Ford agreed to proceed.

That night Joseph's attorneys told him that Governor Ford planned to march to Nauvoo at 8:00 a.m. the next morning. A company of troops was to remain behind to guard the jail and protect the prisoners. These would be selected by the governor from those troops on whose loyalty he could most rely.[124]

In preparation for the march, Justice Smith postdated Joseph's and Hyrum's subpoenas to the hearing on the treason charge an additional two days. He did not advise either Joseph or his attorneys of this change, but the justice was determined to lead his Carthage Greys as a part of the military procession entering Nauvoo in triumph.[125]

At the jail, Hyrum attempted to raise Joseph's spirits by reading Book of Mormon accounts of God delivering his servants from prison.[126] He read the accounts of Alma and Amulek in the prison at Ammonihah, and of Lehi and Nephi in the Lamanite prison. He also spoke of the three Nephites who were delivered from prison by the power of God. "Joseph," he asked, "Don't you believe the Lord can do that for us?"

"Yes, I believe he can," replied the prophet, "but I do not believe he will."

After John Taylor prayed around 9:30, prisoners and guests retired. At our insistence, Joseph and Hyrum occupied the only bed in the room. John Fullmer and Dan Jones lay on the floor.[127] I sat at the table writing the day's events until about midnight, when my last candle flickered out and left me in the dark.[128]

At about that time, a gunshot sounded near the jail,[129] and Joseph rose from his bed. After a moment, he lay on the floor between John Fullmer and Dan Jones. Joseph laid out his right arm and said to Brother Fullmer, "Lay your head on my arm for a pillow, Brother John."

After it was quiet once more, Joseph talked about his foreboding of death. "I would like to see my family again," he said. "I would to God that I could preach to the Saints in

Nauvoo one more time." When Fulimer tried to rally his spirits, Joseph thanked him.[130] Soon after, I retired from my place at the table to the bed Joseph had left. A moment later, Joseph turned to Dan Jones and whispered, "Are you afraid to die?"

Dan asked, "Has it come to that, think you? Engaged in such a cause, I do not think that death could have many terrors."

Joseph then uttered the final prophecy of his life. "You will yet see Wales and fulfill the mission appointed you before you die."[131]

Sometime later, Dan Jones was awakened by heavy footsteps outside the jail. He called us to wakefulness, and then we heard someone outside saying in a hushed voice, "Who? And how many shall go in?" Looking from one of the south windows, Jones saw a large number of men entering the prison, then gave the alarm as they rushed up the stairs. But when the intruders heard us moving about and Joseph yelling, "Come on, assassins! We are ready for you and would as willingly die now as at daylight." they hurriedly left the jail.[132]

At 5:00 a.m. brethren on their way to Nauvoo stopped by with letters and newspapers. After they left, Joseph asked Dan Jones to inquire about the previous night's disturbances. When he descended the stairs and opened the door on the south, he learned that the governor had kept his promise to provide a guard for the protection of the prisoners. This guard, which was to have been selected from among those on "whose loyalty [Ford] could most rely" was none other than the Carthage Greys, whose commanding officer was Robert

Smith. Frank Worrell, as bitter an anti-Mormon as could be found in the county, was sergeant of the guard of seven men then on duty at the jail. He listened to Jones' question and laughed in his face.

"We've had too much trouble bringing Old Joe here to let him ever escape alive," Worrell declared, "and unless you want to die with him, you'd better leave before sundown. You're not a damned bit better than him for taking his part. You'll see that I can prophesy better than Old Joe, for neither he nor his brother, nor anyone who remains with them, will see the sun set today."[133]

When Dan Jones told the Prophet what he had heard, Joseph sent him to inform the governor. On his way to Governor Ford's quarters, Jones heard more threatening talk among the militiamen and another prediction of Joseph's death that day.

Jones, a short, stocky riverboat pilot, approached the governor at the hotel, filled with concern he told Governor Ford what had occurred during the night, what the officer of the guard had said, and what he had heard on his way to the hotel.

Ford listened politely, then said, "You are unnecessarily alarmed for the safety of your friends, sir. The people are not that cruel."[134]

The callous reply of the governor to Jones' warnings filled Jones with great anger. "Governor Ford," he said, "those men are American citizens and have surrendered themselves to your Excellency upon pledging your honor for their safety! I demand of you protection of their lives! If you do not do this, if you do not guard them with someone other than these paid assassins, I have but one more desire, and that is if you leave their lives in the hands of these men to be sacrificed…"

"What is that, sir?" the governor asked.

"It is that the Almighty will preserve my life to a proper time and place, that I may testify that you have been timely warned of their danger."[135] Jones returned to the jail, but the guard refused to let him enter without a pass. Knowing that the governor had given passes to one or two others to come and go, Dan went looking for Ford again. He returned to the Hamilton House, where he found Governor Ford with the troops under Captain Dunn, ready to escort him to Nauvoo.[136]

Ford's plan of the night before to march to Nauvoo with all of the troops from Carthage and Warsaw, except for a guard of the most faithful for the jail, had been abandoned either late the night before, or early that morning. Ford had learned of a plan to get the troops into Nauvoo and there initiate a battle by the simple expedient of having one of the troops or an apostate Mormon take advantage of the darkness to fire on the soldiers. That act of violence could then be blamed on the Mormons and would give the assembled troops sufficient excuse to attack the city. Ford later wrote, "I was satisfied that there were those amongst us fully capable of such an act."[137] If he was assured of sufficient malice among his troops to attack a city of unsuspecting men, women, and children, how could he doubt the willingness of his men to attack the jail where Joseph and Hyrum were prisoners?

Nevdertheless, because of his concerns, Ford ordered the troops to be disbanded, both at Carthage and at Warsaw. He decided to march on Nauvoo with only the troops under Captain Dunn. The disbanded troops at once became a mob of nearly 1700 armed and dangerous men.[138]

When the disbanded troops moved a short distance from the governor, they shouted loudly that they would return and kill Joe and Hyrum as soon as Ford left town. When Jones called these threats to the governor's attention, Ford took no notice, even though it was impossible to avoid hearing them.[139]

At 8:00 a.m. Cyrus Wheelock approached the governor, asking that he and I be given free passage in and out of the jail. "Governor," Mr. Wheelock said, "you must be aware by this time that the prisoners have no fears in relation to any lawful demands made against them. But you have also heard sufficient to justify concern that their enemies would destroy the Smiths if they had them in their power. As I prepare to leave for Nauvoo, I fear for those men, They are safe as regards the law. But they are not sale from the hands of traitors and midnight assassins who thirst for their blood and have determined to spill it. And under these circumstances, I have a heavy heart."

Ford replied, as he often had, with another reminder of his promise of protection and a fair trial.[140] Wheelock did not have much faith in the governor's promise. He returned to the jail with a pass given him by the governor and smuggled a six-shot pepper-box pistol to Joseph, who placed it in the pocket of his coat.[141]

Around 8:20 that morning, Joseph wrote his last letter to Emma. A short time after finishing it, he added a postscript: "Dear Emma, I am very much resigned to my lot, knowing I am justified, and have done the best that could be done. Give my love to the children and all my friends...May God bless you all. Amen."[142]

Meanwhile Captain Dunn and his company were preparing to travel to Nauvoo with Governor Ford. The rest of the militia was disbanded, excepting the two companies of Greys ordered by the governor to stay and guard the jail under the command of Captain Robert Smith.[143]

This was the same Robert Smith who had either ignored or instigated three bitter, bloody threats against the Smiths in the previous two days, and who had tried to set bail of an amount and in a way that were both contrary to Illinois law. Now, as the governor departed for Nauvoo, leaving Joseph and Hyrum in jail contrary to his promise of the day before, he left them under the protection of one of their bitterest enemies, who was in command of militiamen who had demonstrated over and over again their intent to destroy the Mormon leaders.

The Greys had rebelled when Joseph and Hyrum were introduced to the militia in Carthage, and then caused an uproar at the commanding general's quarters when the Smiths and Governor Ford joined him. Then, on the night of Joseph's arrival in Carthage, under the governor's window at the

Hamilton House, the Carthage Greys whooped, yelled, hooted, and cursed, threatening the lives of Joseph and all the Mormons.[144] Never, when in the proximity of Joseph Smith, had the Greys manifested anything less than the utmost hostility. On his way out of Carthage, Governor Ford was stopped by Nauvoo's city marshal, John Greene. The Marshall told Ford of a conspiracy to kill the Smiths during the governor's absence. "Marshal Greene, you are too enthusiastic," said the governor.[145]

Four miles out of town, Colonel Buckmaster, one of the officers in the state militia, told the governor he suspected an attack on the jail.[146] The governor ignored that warning as well. By noon, Governor Ford had been informed of the Smiths' mortal danger by Dan Jones, Cyrus Wheelock, John Greene and Colonel Buckmaster. In addition he had heard disbanded militiamen promise to murder the prophet. Yet he later wrote, "I entertained no suspicion of such an attack; at any rate, none before noon the next day [June 28th]."[147]

When I became ill during lunch, Joseph sent Stephen Markham for something to settle my stomach.[148] Markham had been given a pass by the governor. As Markham returned to jail with medicine, he passed near the encampment of Carthage Greys in the public square. He was stopped there by a man named Stewart and told to get out of town in five minutes or he would be killed. Markham, of course, was the man who did not know what fear was. He was not inclined to be driven anywhere and accordingly refused to depart from Carthage. Stewart then attacked him with a fixed bayonet.

Markham knocked the musket and bayonet aside with his left hand, then pushed the man down with his right. Stewart then called for the Greys, who came running.

The Greys ordered Markham out of town at once, but he refused again. They could kill him, Markham told them, but they would never drive him to a place he did not choose to go. As they threatened Markham with their bayonets, he parried their thrusts, knocking down ten or twelve men with his fists.

The Greys finally crowded Markham so much he couldn't fight. Then Hamilton, the innkeeper, waded into the fray, advising Markham to leave. Over Markham's objections, Hamilton brought his horse. Prodding Markham with bayonets until his boots filled with blood, the Greys forced him onto his horse. Then, forming a hollow square, they marched Stephen Markham into the timber.[149]

The afternoon of the 27th was humid and rainy. We were all depressed. The guards' menacing talk was impossible to ignore, so the pervading spirit was that of discouragement.

In an attempt to cheer us, Elder Taylor sang a song newly popular in Nauvoo, "A Poor Wayfaring Man of Grief." When he finished, Joseph asked him to sing it again.[150]

I had heard the song before, but had never listened closely. I listened now, and the words of the sixth verse seemed to echo the sentiments of my heart and to describe the true purpose for our presence in the Carthage Jail.

*In pris'n I saw him next, condemned*

*To meet a traitor's doom at morn.*
*The tide of lying tongues I stemmed,*
*And honored him 'mid share and scorn.*
*My friendship's utmost zeal to try,*
*He asked if I for him would die.*
*The flesh was weak, my blood ran chill,*
*But my free spirit cried, "I will!"*

The guard changed at 4:00 p.m., leaving only eight men at the jail. The rest of the company remained camped about a quarter of a mile away. All others had been discharged.[151]

Around 5:00, jailer Stigall told us what had happened to Stephen Markham. He then suggested that we would be safer in the jail's main cell. It had narrow slots rather than windows, a barred door, and a strong lock. Because we knew we would be safer there, we agreed to go in after dinner.[152]

As the jailer went out, Joseph turned to me and asked, "If we go into the cell, will you go in with us?"

I was astonished by his question.

"Brother Joseph," I said, "you did not ask me to cross the Mississippi River with you. You did not ask me to come to Carthage with you. You did not ask me to come to jail with you. So do you think I would forsake you now? But I will tell you what I will do: If you are condemned to be hung for treason, I will be hung in your stead, and you shall go free."

Joseph said simply, "You cannot."

But I replied, "I will."[153]

# 8

It was just after this that the mob came out of the woods in the northeast. Elder Taylor, seated on the sill of the east window, gave the alarm. The mob came to the building and through the gate or over the fence. Hearing a discharge of firearms at the front of the building, I glanced around the curtain. Gathered below I saw about 100 men, their faces blackened with water and gunpowder. We know now that the mob was comprised mainly of members of the Warsaw militia,[154] who had been incited to attack the jail by a speech given to them at Golden Point by Thomas Sharp, editor of the *Warsaw Signal*.

I watched as the guard of Greys pretended to protect us against our attackers. They fired blank cartridges[155] over the heads of the mob and stepped aside.

There was a great clatter of musketry in the stairwell. Immediately Joseph, Hyrum, John Taylor and I leaped to the door and put our weight against it.[156] The door had no lock or latch of any kind to secure it. Then someone tried forcing the door and, thinking it locked, fired a ball above the keyhole.[157] The ball passed harmlessly between us. We recognized at once that the door was no protection. The passage of the ball through the wood had not seemed to impede its progress in the least.

While John Taylor, Joseph, and I sprang aside, Hyrum stayed against the door, trying to hold it with his leg, his shoulder, his arm, and his head. A second ball fired through the door struck him in the left side of his nose, passing into the brain. He staggered back across the room and collapsed. As he fell, another ball fired through the east window hit him in the back, passed through his body, and pulverized the watch in his vest pocket. Falling, he exclaimed, "I am a dead man."

As Hyrum lay on the floor before the door, he was shot an additional two times. One ball grazed his breast and entered his head at his throat. Another ball struck his left leg.[158]

With great tenderness, Joseph knelt next to Hyrum. "Oh! My poor, dear brother Hyrum!" he cried out. Then he arose and took the six-shooter left by Cyrus Wheelock from his pocket. Opening the door slightly and reaching around the casing, Joseph aimed at the stairwell, now filled with men, and snapped the trigger six times. The gun only fired three times,[159] but three men fell wounded.[160]

There have been those who have said that Joseph Smith was no martyr because he fired a gun in his own defense. I do not care much about what people call Joseph, for I know myself what he was. But it is important to recognize that if Joseph had not fired the gun when he did, no one in the jailer's bedroom would have survived. The mob would have rushed into the chamber and killed us all, as was clearly their intention.

As it was, firing the gun slowed the mob's rush up the stairway. They were not anxious to come into the room where weapons might await. However, balls continued to enter through the east window, lodging in the ceiling above Hyrum's head.[161]

Meanwhile, the men on the landing outside the door, wearing their demonic expressions and screaming horrid oaths,[162] began to reach around the casing of the door left-handed, discharging their guns through the partially open door. But John Taylor had picked up Stephen Markham's walking stick. He parried the muzzles being thrust through the entryway. In that way he protected us for several moments.

But Elder Taylor knew that in the absence of any more gun fire from within, the mob was certain to rush into the room at any moment. Nothing but cowardice had kept them outside thus far. With no hope of protection within, John Taylor hoped there might be friends or chance of escape outside. He rushed to the east window, fifteen to twenty feet above the ground, but as he was at the point of leaping out, a ball from the doorway pierced his left thigh, struck a bone or a nerve and completely, if only momentarily, paralyzed him. But his momentum carried him to the window, where he was nearly on a balance, but tilting slowly outward and unable to stop himself. As he began falling through the open window, he saw below him fifty men with guns and bayonets, waiting.

One man, unwilling to wait, aimed at Elder Taylor and fired a ball into the vest pocket over his heart. It struck the watch he carried there and stopped it at exactly 5:16 and 26 seconds. The force of the ball knocked him back into the room. The shot almost certainly saved his life.

When he found he could move again, Taylor crawled across the floor and under the bed, which offered the only possibility of protection in that part of the room. But now, with the door open, he could be seen quite clearly lying on his face under the edge of the bed with his head toward the east wall. Taylor was shot three more times. One ball entered his left calf. Another entered his left wrist, passing into his hand. The third hit him in the fleshy part of the hip, tearing away a piece of flesh the size of my fist and dashing the mangled fragments against the wall.[163]

While most of the mob continued to fire at Taylor, others attempted to reach Joseph and I, who stood at the front of the room to the side of the door. By extending their guns around the doorjamb, they blindly pointed their discharges at the corner of the room where we had retreated. I recommenced my attack with the walking stick, trying to protect Taylor and Joseph.[164]

Joseph, who had stood behind me in the corner (the safest part of the room, if any part could be called safe), now suddenly stepped out. Calmly walking to the middle of the room, he dropped his pistol near the body of Hyrum. Then, determined to try and save the lives of his brethren in the room, Joseph sprang for the window. But as he reached it, two balls pierced him from the door and one entered his right breast from below. As he toppled out the window, he spoke his final words, "O Lord, my God!"[165]

As Joseph's feet went out the window, I was immediately behind him. Balls were whistling all around me. I was halfway out the window, determined to see the end of this man I loved. He hit the ground on his head and shoulder. I checked my rush.[166]

Instantly, someone on the landing yelled, "He's leaped the window!" There was an immediate dash of the mob from the stairs and entryway to prevent his possible escape.[167]

There were now a hundred bayonets below, and more coming at every moment. I watched for some seconds, unnoticed by the men below in their madness to see if the prophet showed any signs of life. At last, fully satisfied that Joseph was dead, I turned and moved quickly to the prison door at the head of the stairs to see if it was open.

When I reached the door, Taylor called out, "Stop, Doctor, and take me along." But I pressed my way until I found the prison doors unbarred, then instantly returned. Taking Taylor under my arm, I rushed by the stairs and into the protection of the prison cell next door.[168]

Kneeling over Taylor in the halflight, grief nearly overcame me. "Oh Brother Taylor," I said, "is it possible that they have killed Brother Hyrum and Joseph? Surely, it cannot be. Yet I saw them shot." Then I prayed three times, "Oh Lord, my God, spare thy servants!"

I dragged Brother Taylor further into the cell, covered him with a filthy mattress in the hope of hiding him, and said, "This is a hard case to lay you on the floor. But if your wounds are not fatal, I want you to live to tell the story."

I then returned to the doorway of the jailer's bedroom and stood before it. I listened to the sounds of gunfire and celebration outside the east window where the mob had propped the Prophet Joseph against the well, and waited for the return of the mob, expecting at any moment to be shot.[169]

Suddenly I heard a loud cry from the open doorway at the bottom of the stairs: "The Mormons are coming!" Of course it was not true, but the threat of 5,000 armed men was more than enough. The murderers fled into the woods, the little band clearly no match for the enraged and powerful Nauvoo Legion they expected. It was then, as I listened to the diminishing sounds of the mob in full retreat, that I began to understand that I was not going to die. But I could not understand. It seemed an unimaginable mistake. Joseph, dead by the well; Hyrum, dead on the floor beside me; John Taylor, shot to doll rags and probably dead, lying under a filthy mattress in the cell. And Willard...

I had a drop of blood on my left ear and a burn mark on my neck where a ball had grazed me as I stood at the window, but I was without so much as a hole in my garments.[170] I could not understand why these wonderful men should have suffered so, when I was left alive and uninjured. It seemed to me a most awful miscarriage of divine justice.

Then, quietly, powerfully, I remembered the words Joseph had spoken to me just over a year before: "Willard, the time will come when bullets will fly around you like hail. You will see friends fall to the right and to the left of you. But there shall not be so much as a hole in your garment."[171]

Still it seemed impossible that they had been taken. There in the bedroom of the Carthage Jail I asked the Lord to help me understand, but no answer came that day.

The answer came later, and not just to me, but to all of those thousands who had loved and revered the Prophet and the Patriarch.

In part it came from Brigham Young, who some time later said: "The Lord never let a prophet fall to the earth until he had accomplished his work. Taking Joseph and Hyrum away was the greatest blessing God could bestow. They had suffered enough."[172]

The answer also came from Lucy, the mother of the martyrs. When I sent word to Nauvoo the evening of June 27 about the deaths of Joseph and Hyrum, Lucy began to prepare herself to see her sons. She braced every nerve, roused the very energy of her soul, and called continuously upon God to strengthen her.

Even so, on the morning of June 29 as she was ushered into the Mansion House and saw her murdered sons before her, Lucy sank back and cried out in agony, "My God, my God, why hast thou forsaken this family!"

Lucy received an answer as a voice spoke to her, saying, "I have taken them unto Myself that they might have rest."

And then she remembered a promise about her sons that she had received through the Spirit in Missouri, a promise that in five years Joseph would have power over all his enemies. Understanding came to her with the gentle comfort of the Spirit. The time had elapsed, and the promise was fulfilled.[173]

# NOTES

1. Richards, Preston D, "Willard Richards The Martyrdom of Joseph and Hyrum Smith." *The Improvement Era,* Vol. 10, June 1907, p. 564.

2. Smith, Joseph. *Documentary History of the Church,* Vol. 5, pp. 40, 41. Hereafter cited as *DHC.*

3. *Ibid.,* p. 41.

4. D. Michael Quinn, "They Served: The Richards Legacy in the Church." *The Ensign*, Vol. X, Jan. 1980, p. 25; Noall, Claire, *Intimate Disciple,* University of Utah Press, Salt Lake City, 1957, pp. 101, 102.

5. *Intimate Disciple,* p. 104.

6. Richards, Preston D., p. 562.

7. Brooks, Melvin R., *LDS Reference Encyclopedia, Bookcraft,* Inc. Salt Lake City, 1960, p. 421.

8. *DHC*, Vol. 2, p. 492.

9. Richards, Preston D., p. 563.

10. Whitney, Orson F., *Life of Heber* C. *Kimball,* Bookcraft, Inc., Salt Lake City, 1967, pp. 143, 144.

11. *Doctrine and Covenants* 118:6. Hereafter cited as D&C.

12. Flake, Lawrence R., *Mighty Men of Zion,* Deseret Press, Salt Lake City, 1974, pp. 123-124.

13. *Intimate Disciple,* pp. 306, 307; Barrett, Ivan J., *Joseph Smith and the Restoration* (1st Edition), Brigham Young University Press, Provo, Utah, 1968, p. 425.

14. *Journal History of the Church of Jesus Christ of Latter-day Saints,* November 21, 1841.

15. *DHC,* Vol. 6, p. 619.

16. *DHC,* Vol. 6, p. 546.

17. Taylor, John, *The Martyrdom of Joseph Smith,* pp. 14, 15. The account I have used is published as an introduction in Daniel Tyler's *A Concise History of the Mormon Battalion.*

18. Cummings, Horace, *The Contributor,* Salt Lake City, Vol. 5, pp. 251-260.

19. Law was appointed by revelation in D&C 124: 91.

20. *DHC,* Vol. 6, p. 438.

21. *DHC,* Vol. 7, p. 227.

22. Gregg, Thomas, *The Prophet of Palmyra,* (Title page missing. Copy in library at Brigham Young University), pp. 505, 506.

23. *DHC.* Vol. 6, p. 375.

24. Taylor, John, *The Martyrdom of Joseph Smith,* p. 15.

25. Letter from Sydney Rigdon to Governor Ford. *DHC,* Vol. 6, p. 470.

26. *DHC,* Vol. 6, p. 446.

27. For an excellent discussion of the legality and the implications of the abatement of the *Expositor,* see

Oaks, Dallin H., "Suppression of the Nauvoo Expositor," *Utah Law Review,* IX, 1965, p. 875. Also, DHC, Vol. 6, p. 447.

28. Roberts, B. H., Comprehensive History of the Church, Brigham Young University Press, Provo, Utah, 1965, Vol. 2, p. 230. Also, *DHC,* Vol. 6, p. 447.

29. Taylor, John, *The Martyrdom of Joseph Smith,* p. 18.

30. *Warsaw Signal,* Warsaw, Illinois, June 12, 1844, p. 2.

31. *Ibid.*

32. *DHC,* Vol. 6, p. 516; also Introduction to Vol. 6, p. xxxix.

33. *Ibid.,* p. 454.

34. *DHC,* Vol. 6, p. 516.

35. *Ibid.,* p. 454.

36. *Ibid.,* p. 456-458.

37. *Ibid.,* p. 464.

38. *Ibid.,* p. 471, 510, 511, etc.

39. Anson Call, *The Life and Record of Anson Call, Commenced in 1839,* typescript in possession of author, p. 10.

40. *Ibid.,* p. 479.

41. *Ibid.,* pp. 487-491 for the minutes of this trial.

42. *Ibid.,* p. 497.

43. About 500 men. Barrett, Ivan J., *Joseph Smith and the Restoration,* 2nd Edition, p. 493.

44. *DHC,* Vol. 6, p. 480.

45. *Ibid.,* p. 521.

46. *Ibid.,* p. 552.

47. Taylor, John, pp. 24, 25.

48. *DHC,* Vol. 6, pp. 436-437.

49. Taylor, John, pp. 26, 27.

50. *Ibid.,* p. 27.

51. *Ibid.,* p. 28.

52. *DHC,* Vol. 6, p. *536* (533-537).

53. *Ibid.,* Vol. 5, p. 85, 86 for one of the Rocky Mountain prophecies. Also Call, Anson, p. 10. *DHC,* Vol. 6, pp. 545, 546.

54. *Ibid.,* Vol. 6, p. 548.

55. *Millennial Star,* XXIV, p. 333. Hereafter cited as *MS.*

56. Barrett, Ivan J., p. 496.

57. *DHC,* Vol. 6, p. 549; see also the letter from Vilate Kimball to Heber C. Kimball, commenced June 9, 1844. Vilate discusses the impact on Nauvoo of Joseph fleeing the city. "Some were tried almost to death to think Joseph should leave them in the hour of danger. Hundreds have left the city since the fuss first commenced."

58. *DHC* Vol. 6, p. 549.

59. *Ibid.*

60. *DHC* Vol. 5, p. 259.

61. *DHC* Vol. 6, p. 58.

62. *MS* XXIV, p. 333.

63. *Ibid.* pp. 333, 334.

64. *DHC* Vol. 6, p. 540.

65. Cannon, George Q., *Joseph Smith's Life and Work,* p. 472.

66. *DHC* Vol. 6, p. 551.

67. *Ibid.,* pp. 551, 552.

68. *Ibid.,* p. 552.

69. *Ibid.,* p. 553.

70. Jones, Dan. *The Martyrdom of Joseph and Hyrum Smith.* This document, 26 pages in length, was written and submitted at the request of Church historians George A. Smith and Thomas Bullock. The passage quoted is on pages 2 and 3. A copy of this document is in the Appendix.

71. *MS* XXIV, p. 342.

72. *Ibid.,* p. 555.

73. *Ibid.*

74. D&C 135:4.

75. *MS* XXIV, p. 343.

76. *DHC,* Vol. 6, p. 558.

77. *The Life of Mosiah Hancock,* Provo, Utah, Brigham Young University Library Special Collections, p. 28.

78. *Ibid.,* p. 29.

79. *DHC,* Vol. 6, p. 559.

80. *Ibid.*

81. *Ibid.*

82. *Ibid.* pp. 559, 560.

83. Cyrus Wheelock to Geroge A. Smith, December 29, 1854. The passage referred to is also quoted by Dean

C. Jessee in "Return to Carthage: Writing the History of the Martyrdom." *Journal of Mormon History,* Vol. 8, 1981, p. 9.

84. *DHC* Vol. 6, p. 536.

85. Oaks, Dallin H. and Marvin S. Hill, *Carthage Conspiracy: The Trial of the Accused Assassins of Joseph Smith,* University of Illinois Press, 1979, p. 18.

86. *Ibid.,* p. 19.

87. *DHC* Vol. 6, p. 563.

88. Roberts, B. H., *The Rise and Fall of Nauvoo,* Bookcraft, Salt Lake City, 1965, pp. 300, 301.

89. *Journal History,* June 25, 1844.

90. For an excellent treatment of this prophecy and its fulfillment, see Roberts, B. H., "Fulfilled Prophecy: New Evidence of Divine Inspiration in the Prophet Joseph Smith." *Improvement Era,* Vol. XIX, February 1916, pp. 289-294.

91. *DHC* Vol. 6, p. 566.

92. *Ibid.,* p. 567.

93. Cyrus Wheelock to George A. Smith. See Dean Jessee, "Return to Carthage," in *Journal of Mormon History,* Vol. 8, 1981, p. 7.

94. Oaks, Dallin H., *Carthage Conspiracy,* p. 18.

95. *DHC* Vol. 6, pp. 569, 570.

96. *Times and Seasons,* Vol. 5, No. 12, July 1, 1844.

97. Ibid. Also, Ford, Thomas, *History of Illinois,* p. *338.* Cited also in Roberts, B. H., *The Rise and Fall of Nauvoo,* p. 305.

98. Taylor, John, *The Martyrdom of Joseph Smith,* p. 35.

99. *Ibid.,* p. 36.

100. *DHC,* Vol. 6, pp. 555, 556.

101. Roberts, B. H., *The Rise and Fall of Nauvoo,* p. 304.

102. *DHC,* Vol. 6, p. 574.

103. *Ibid.*

104. *Ibid.,* p. 592.

105. Taylor, John, *The Martyrdom of Joseph Smith,* p. 39.

106. *Ibid.,* p. 43.

107. *Ibid.,* p. 41.

108. *Ibid.*

109. *Ibid.*

110. *Ibid.,* p. 42.

111. *Ibid.,* p. 44.

112. *DHC* Vol. 6, p. 566.

113. The editor was George T. M. Davis of the *Alton Telegraph.* His comment is quoted in Oaks, Dallin H., *Carthage Conspiracy,* p. 19, 114. *DHC* Vol. 6, p. 592.

115. *Ibid.*

116. *Ibid.,* p. 594.

117. Pierce, Frederick, *Route from Liverpool to Great Salt Lake Valley,* Liverpool, Farnklin D. Richards, 1855, p. 64.

118. *Historical Record,* a monthly periodical published by Andrew Jenson. Vol. 5-8; or *Church Encyclopedia,* Book 1, p. 566.

119. Taylor, John, *The Martyrdom of Joseph Smith,* p. 45.

120. Nibley, Preston, *Joseph Smith the Prophet,* Salt Lake City, Deseret News Press, 1944, p. 547.

121. Oaks, Dallin H., *Carthage Conspiracy,* p. 19.

122. *Ibid.*

123. *Ibid.*

124. *DHC* Vol. 6, pp. 599, 600.

125. *Ibid.,* p. 600. See also B. H. Roberts' *The Rise and Fall of Nauvoo,* p. 307.

126. *DHC* Vol. 6, p. 600.

127. Taylor, John, *The Martyrdom of Joseph Smith,* p. 46.

128. Roberts, B. H., *The Rise and Fall of Nauvoo,* p. 307.

129. *DHC* Vol. 6, p. 600.

130. *Ibid.,* p. 601.

131. *Ibid.* On August 28, 1844, Dan Jones left for a mision to Great Britain and was assigned to the land of his birth—Wales. In four years of service he baptized about 4,000 people. See B. H. Roberts,

*The Rise and Fall of Nauvoo,* p. 308, and the *L.D.S. Reference Encyclopedia*, p. 154.

132. Jones, Dan, *The Martyrdom of Joseph and Hyrum Smith,* p. 10.

133. *DHC* Vol. 6, p. 602.

134. Jones, Dan, *The Martyrdom of Joseph arid Hyrum Smith,* p. 11.

135. *Ibid.,* p. 12.

136. *Ibid.*

137. *DHC* Vol. 7, pp. 14, 15.

138. *Ibid.,* p. 14.

139. *Ibid.,* Vol. 6, pp. 603, 604.

140. *Ibid.,* pp. 604, 607.

141. *Ibid.,* p. 607.

142. *Ibid.,* p. 605.

143. *Ibid.,* p. 606. Also, Vol. 7, p. 17.

144. *DHC* Vol. 7, p. 19, footnote.

145. *Ibid.,* Vol. 6, p. 611.

146. *Ibid.,* Vol. 7, p. 22.

147. *Ibid.*

148. *Ibid.,* Vol. 6, p. 614.

149. Correspondence from Stephen Markham to Wilford Woodruff, June 20, 1856.

150. *DHC* Vol. 6, pp. 614, 615.

151. *Ibid.,* pp. 615, 616.

152. *Ibid.,* p. 616.

153. *Ibid.*

154. *Ibid.* p. 606, and Vol. 7, p. 31.

155. *Ibid.,* Vol. 7, p. 31. See also Barnes, Dr. Thomas L., "Carthage Jail Physician Testifies." *The Pioneer,* Vol. VI, #1, Spring 1954, p. 51.

156. Taylor, John, *The Martyrdom of Joseph Smith,* p. 48.

157. *DHC* Vol. 6, p. 617.

158. *Ibid.*

159. Taylor, John, *The Martyrdom of Joseph Smith,* p. 49.

160. *DHC* Vol. 7, p. 31. According to William M. Daniels, two of the three were mortally wounded. (see *A Correct Account of the Murder of Generals Joseph and Hyrum* Smith, *at Carthage, on the 27th Day of June, 1844, Nauvoo,* 1845, p. 11.)

161. *Ibid.,* Vol. 6, p. 617.

162. Taylor, John, *The Martyrdom of Joseph and Hyrum Smith,* pp. 49, 50.

163. *Ibid.,* pp. 50, 51.

164. *DHC* Vol. 6, p. 620.

165. *Ibid.,* p. 618.

166. Correspondence, Jennetta Richards to Rev. John Richards (her father) and her brothers and sisters, July 8, 1844.

167. *DHC* Vol. 6, pp. 620, 621.

168. *Ibid.,* p. 621.

169. Taylor, John, *The Martyrdom of Joseph Smith,* p. 51; DHC Vol. 6, p. 621.

170. McGavin, Cecil, *Nauvoo the Beautiful*, Salt Lake City, Stevens and Wallace, Inc., 1946, p. 154.
171. *DHC*, Vol. 6, p. 619.
172. McGavin, Cecil, *Nauvoo The Beautiful*, p. 154.
173. Smith, Lucy Mack, *History of the Prophet Joseph Smith by His Mother,* Salt Lake City, Bookcraft, 1969, pp. 324, 325.

# APPENDIX

(This account preserves original spelling and grammar. It should be noted that this narrative was written while Dan Jones was serving as Mission President in Wales and without access to documents that might have assisted him in his recollections.)

## THE MARTYRDOM OF
# JOSEPH AND HYRUM SMITH

by Dan Jones
January 20, 1855

June 12, 1844—While Joseph Smith was standing by the side of his brother Hyrum, along with several other friends on the portico of the Mansion House, Nauvoo, awaiting the remains of my little son, 3 1/2 years of age, who had died there to be brought out to be buried, and when he was about stepping into a carriage he was accosted by the Sheriff of Hancock County with a writ to appear before a Magistrate, Smith, in Carthage, charged with destroying the Press of the "Nauvoo Expositor;" he expostulated in vain for the privilege of paying the last debt of honor to the remains of the sacred dead. A few days previously depositions were taken by Mr.

Smith, of men from Carthage, who deposed that a band of men residing at Carthage had colleagues with some of the owners of the above Press to decoy him to Carthage with the intention of assassinating him. Those affidavits were sent to Gov. Ford with a request for protection, which failing to arrive in time of need, advantage was taken of the writ where it allows to appear before the issuer "or any other Magistrate in the County," by demanding a trial before Justice D. H. Wells, where he was honorably acquitted. In a few days however another Sheriff was sent with another warrant for the same offence, demanding him to go to Carthage; but the duty of self preservation, with the entreaties of many friends delayed his going, and expresses were sent to the Governor who, upon hearing of the assemblage of several thousand of the mob at Carthage repaired there, and was prevailed upon by the mob, as he himself subsequently admitted in public, to send a possee Committattus to bring Mr. Smith to Carthage who, arriving at his house Saturday evening were respectfully received and entertained at Mr. Smith's own table, with the best that the place afforded, as was also their horses fed. Having heard that he would be waylaid and shot in the dark if he went out that night Mr. Smith requested the possee to stay with him until morning, but they returned to the mob, and excited them by fabulous tales of hairs breadth escapes, &c.

Sunday 23—Another possee demanded him and tendered Governor Ford's "honour" as pledge for his safety; but Mr. Smith sent to inform him that he would come out next day, and remained with his bro. Hyrum and others in Council. The assembled thousands at the Grove, alike was the fair city of Nauvoo on that solemn day enwrapped in sable robes of despair—all felt as if their much loved Prophet was already beyond the vail; nor could the hiding folds of night's dark cloak cheer their throbbing hearts with a beam of hope; but the pensive morrows sun saw a City bathed in tears, and after a night as sleepless to the devoted Saints below as it was to those sleepless on high recording their prayers and sealing up the "vials."

Monday 24th—Eventfull day! found hundreds gathered before the Mansion House early in the morning:—in their midst with head erect towering above the rest the Prophet stood gazing alternately on the devoted City and its much loved citizens; in suspense he listened to the entreaties of the throng, not to give himself up or he would be murdered; a few, tho' enough, brave hearted men proposed to escort him where he would find the protection denied him by the "Christians" among the red "pagans" of the West:—others, up north would have him go, while a fearless Tar, inured to other climes, whose heart was a Malstrom of fury, proffered him a safe passage on a Steam Boat, then ready by, to whither he would; a smile of approbation lit up the Seer's countenance,—his lively boys hanging on to his skirts urged on the suite and cryed "Father, O Father don't go to Carthage they will kill you. "—a volley of arguments more powerfull yet from the streaming eyes of her he loved best, and whose embrace was hard to sever; nor least impressive were the pleadings of his doting Mother whose grey ringlets honored a head weather-beaten by the persecutions of near twice ten years, "My Son, my Son, can you leave me without promising to return? Some forty times before have I seen you from me dragged, but never before without saying you would return; what say you now my Son? He stood erect like a beacon among roaring breakers—his gigantic mind grasping still higher; the fire flashed in his eye; with hand uplifted on high he spoke "My friends, nay dearer still my brethren, I love you, I love the City of Nauvoo too well to save my life at your expense,—if I go not to them they will come and act out the horrid Missouri scenes in Nauvoo;—I may prevent it, I fear not death, my work is well nigh done, keep the faith and I will die for Nauvoo. So said the Prophet as he mounted his steed, and together with his brother Hyrum and some 30 or 40 more who chose to follow, they ascended the hill; when near the sacred spot—the Temple, he paused, he looked with admiration first on that, then on the City ere it receded from view in the flats below and remarked, this is the loveliest place and the best people under the heavens, little do they know the trials that await them. While on the prairie we met some messengers previously sent to Carthage who had but just been liberated from prison. When within 4 miles of Carthage we met a company of horseman commanded by Captain Dunn; when they hove in sight Mr. Smith halted his "major" (steed) in the midst of the road and said "brethren you have come far enough; do notfurther expose your lives, stand aloof, let all their vengeance be wreaked upon my head, I am going like a lamb to the slaughter with a conscience void of offence. At this time Mr. Wood, his Counsell, rode in front of the Company to know their intentions and soon returned with an order from the Governor for all the State arms which were Nauvoo. When signal of acceptance was given they advanced and Mr. Smith addressed them after endorsing the order, declaring his innocence of the charges preferred against him and demanded of them as an American Citizen to defend his life until he should have an investigation, to which Capt. Dunn reply'd that he would protect him at the risk of his own life, then turning to his men asked "What say you, boys, will you stand by me to see Mr. Smith have justice?" The response was by three cheers; and we all returned to Nauvoo, got all the arms, and in the evening the Company returned and arrived at Carthage late at night failing to get a horse I remained in the City.

25th—Documents of importance for the trial being in Mrs. Smith's possession, by request I took them out to Carthage and arrived during the trial of Mr. Smith and the City Council and in time to give in my evidence, which was admitted to be not the least important in their favour. There I heard Wilson Law, in endeavoring to get a warrant against Mr. Smith for Treason, declare that in preaching from Daniel II, 44, Smith had said that the kingdom referred to therein was already set up, and that he (Mr. Smith) was the King over it! Wonder if Daniel himself was not most treasonable for predicting it? The defendants having given bail to appear at the quarter sessions were released and returned to Nauvoo; but before Mr. Smith could leave I went down stairs in Hamiltons Hotel where I overheard the leaders of the mob say that they did not expect to prove anything against him, but that they had eighteen accusations against him, and that as one failed they would try another to detail him there. One of them, by the name of Jackson, reply'd when I told them to desist from their cruel persecutions that they had worked too hard to get old Joe to Carthage to let him get out of it alive, and pointing to his pistols said, "The balls are in there that will decide his case." I repaired upstairs and informed Mr. Smith what threats I had heard, when he informed me "They are going to take me to prison without a guard; you will not leave me will you?" to which I reply'd that I had come to die with him the rather. He took me aside into the front room and asked "Have you anything with you?" One little bulldog I reply'd, and this switch, pointing to a black hickory club in my hand, the which parryed the rifles of the assassins in prison by Mr. Taylor. Let me have the first said he, which was no sooner said than safely deposited where I wished a dozen more to be. Now the rush of heavy treads up the stairs drew out attention and the stentorian voice of an officer demanding the prisoners, when Dr. Willard Richards met him in the door which was actually too narrow for any but himself to pass. Mr. Reid, their Counsell, also Mr. Taylor, Hyrum Smith, Judge Phelps, Col. Markam and all remonstrated against such an unnecessary exposition of the defendant lives until they desisted. It was then that Justice Smith made out a mittimus, and the "Carthage Grays" escorted them to prison. Being dark, Mr. Smith asked me to get inside somehow, and Col. Markam on one side, with a hickory club, while I was on the other, outside the guard, I parry'd off the guns and bayonets of the drunken rabble who tried to break the ranks to stab them; the prison doors being open before a light was produced I rushed between the guard and the door and forced my way into the farthest cells unhindered, followed by the defendants and the above named, except Judge Phelps, who remained (I think) at Hamiltons; Mr. Reid also, but some few other bretheren were with us with whom I was not personally acquainted until then; but it will be a long time ere I forget

The first night in Carthage cells with the Prophet and the Patriarch!

Amusing conversation on various interesting topics engaged us till late; after prayer, which made Carthage prison into the gate of heaven for awhile, we lay promiscuously on the floor, the last words spoken were, by the Prophet,— "For the most intelligent dream tonight bretheren;" and the first words spoken next morning were by him also enquiring for the same. None, save one were told which was listened to by all as follows— "Portrayed before my mind was Gov. Ford and troops on their way across the prairie to Nauvoo, the prisoners had plead in vain to return with him, although promised by him to go; with a letter of importance I saw myself driven from Carthage, galloping through the masses of medley soldiers, half Indians and semi barbarians, I hurried across the prairie, had gone downon a boat from Nauvoo towards Quincy, but landed at Warsaw awoke, in midst of powder, smoke, death, and carnage." The Prophet reply'd it was ominous of future events not did he believe the Governor would ever take him to Nauvoo alive.

After breakfast we were removed to an upstairs room the entrance to which was up a flight of stairs from the front prison door, which was guarded by soldiers, by alternate four hours; the door was of pine, common batton, without bolts, lock, or even a latch that would shut; on the south side were two large windows, and one on the East, a tier of cells lead from the North, while the entrance was at the N. West corner. Its furniture consisted of a bedstead, chair or two, and some mattresses.

During the forenoon we were visited by Judge Phelps, J. P. Green, J. S. Fullmore, and C. H. Wheelock, the last I think brought a revolver in his boot, and left it with the prisoners when he retired; most of my forenoon's work consisted in hewing, with my penknife, a wharped door to get it on the latch, and in preparing to fortify against a night attack, in which Col. Markam was also industrious. The Prophet appeared extremely anxious by his injunction to the messengers who left for Nauvoo, among whom were Dr. Brenhisel, I think, to send out testimonies to exonerate his brother Hyrum. A portion of us were alternately preaching to the guards, at which the Prophet, Patriarch and all took turns and several were relieved before their time was out because they admitted they were proselyted to the belief of the innocency of the prisoners, which rendered them incompetent of guarding! Frequently they admitted they had been imposed upon by the tales of the mobs, and more than once was it heard "Let us go home boys for I will not fight against these men." Hyrum showed an ardent devotion to the Prophet, every way encourageing him to believe that the Lord for His Church's sake would release him to their service, while Joseph reply'd, "Could my brother Hyrum be but liberated it would not matter so much about me; poor Rigdon, I am glad he has gone to Pittsburgh out of the way, were he to preside, in less than five years he would lead the Church to destruction." He entertained us much by the recital of two dreams the which he had received not long before, one in which he saw himself pitched into a dry well by Wm. and Wilson Law who had previously tied his hands behind him; while struggling to get up and near the top he discovered Wilson tackled by a ferocious wild beast in an adjoining wood, crying for his help while nearer to him still was William with outstretched tongue; blue in the face, and the green poison forced out of his mouth by the coiling of a huge serpent around his body, relaxing its embrace occasionally and thereby enabling him to cry aloud "Oh brother Joseph come and save me or I die." To which he reply'd as he had done to a similiar request from his brother Wilson, "I cannot, for you have tied my hands behind me." Ere long however his guide finding him there released and comforted the Prophet while the others met the just retribution of their demerit.

Another time he had seen himself on a lee shore in a heavy storm saving a ship from wrecking by wadeing through the foaming surf and leading her out to the open sea; again the reckless mariners on board rushed into dangerous breakers in despite of his commands from on shore to them to beat off to sea. Again he stemmed the raging seas, now and anon overwhelmed in the foam, with a mighty effort he sprang to the surface, the raging elements hushed at his command, and as on a sea of glass he marched with the patriarch by his side until in the offing he recognized his brother Samuel, light as a fairy, skipping o'er the main;—but the sequel forgotten by me may be remembered by others; the interpretation he gave, I believe, was the stranding of the great ship "Uncle Sam" owing to rejecting a safe Pilot. Their walking on the tranquil ocean donated their triumphs beyond the vail, Samuel's sudden exit after his bretheren solves the only mystery which the Prophet did not unravel, but sure it is that he gave frequent intimations that he would soon gain his liberty, and soar on high beyond the "rage of mobs and angry strife."

Governor Ford and the prisoners Counsell visited them, and at the close of a lengthy appeal from the Prophet, in which he denied the charges preferred against him, and plead for the protection of his life from mob violence until he could prove himself so, which appeared to make but little impression upon His Excellency beyond a verbal promise that he should have justice, and that his friends present, agreeably to his request should visit him, His Excellency promised to take them with him to Nauvoo, which promise he afterwards recalled through fear of the mobs. Dr. Richards was busily engaged writing as dictated by the Prophet. Elder Taylor amused him by singing &c.

About the middle of the afternoon the Sheriff came to take the prisoners to the Courthouse to be tried, Followed by drunken mobs armed and threatening; an altercation ensued between him and the Prison Keeper, because, as was proved by the mittimus to the latter that the prisoners having been placed with him for "safe keeping," were not under the jurisdiction of the former; whereupon the former rushed upstairs and threatened to enforce obedience had not the latter ordered him off his premises until he produced authority to enter. The bretheren named remonstrated with the parties to await the decision of the Counsel who were not present but sent for. In the meantime Mr. Smith seeing the mob gathering and assuming a threatening aspect concluded it best to go with them then, and putting on his hat, followed by allowed by all of us, walked boldly into their midst, politely locked arms with the worst mobocrat he could see, whereas Hyrum paterned after him by clenching the next worse one, followed by Elders Richards and Taylor escorted by a guard, but the mobocrats side was the best protection from the levelled rifles of the surrounding bush hiders, Col. Markam on one side, myself on

the other, with our "switchers" parry'd off the crowding rabble, and after ascending no the Court House much exertion
was made by the mob to proceed forthwith with trial without
letting the defendant have their witnesses, and as soon as they
were overruled, and the trial postponed until next day, the
only Justice in the place, the Smith before spoken of, who
could grant subpeonas for witnesses, absconded until a late
hour, as it purposely to prevent the appearing of the defendants witnesses, and in keeping with the conviction expressed
by them the previous day "That the law cannot touch him, but
that powder and ball will." In the evening they were again
escorted to the prison amidst the whooping, hallooing and
denunciations of enfuriated thousands; while some tauntingly
upbraided him for not calling a legion of angels to release
him, and to destroy his enemies, inasmuch as he pretended to
have a miraculous power; others asked him to prophesy when
and what manner of death awaited him, professing themselves to know all about it; in fact one was forcibly reminded
of the taunting and jeering of the Jews to our holy and meek
Redeemer, so similar did their words and actions prove their
spirits to be.

During the evening the Patriarch read and commented
upon copious extracts from the Book of Mormon, the impris-
onments and deliverance of the servants of God for the
Gospels sake; Joseph bore a powerful testimony to the guards
of the divine authenticity of the Book of Mormon—the
restoration of the Gospel, the administration of angels, and

that the Kingdom of God was again upon the Earth, for the sake of which he was at that time incarcerated in that prison, and not because he had violated any law of God or of man.

Late, we retired to rest, Joseph and Hyrum on the only bedstead while 4 or 5 lay side by side on mattresses on the floor, Dr. Richards sitting up writing until his last candle left him in the dark; the report of a gun, fired close by, caused Joseph whose head was by a window, to arise, leave the bed and lay himself by my side in close embrace; soon after Dr. Richards retired to the bed and while I thought all but myself and heaven asleep, Joseph asked in a whisper of I was afraid to die. "Has that time come think you? Engaged in such a cause I do not think that death would have many terrors," I replied. "You will see Wales and fulfill the mission appointed you ere you die" he said. I believed his word and relied upon it through trying scenes which followed. All the conversation evinced a presentiment of an approaching crisis. At midnight I was awoke by heavy treads as of soldiery close by, and I heard a whispering "Who, and how many shall go in?" under our window; upon arising I saw a large number of men in front of the prison, and gave the alarm as they rushed up stairs to our room door; we had taken the precaution to fortify ourselves by placing a chair, the only defence, against the door, which one of the brethren seized for a weapon, and we stood by the door awaiting their entrance; hearing us they hesitated; when the Prophet with a "Prophets voice" called out" Come on ye assassins we are ready for you, and would as willing die now as at daylight." Hearing this they retired again, and consulted, advanced and retreated alternately, evidently failing to agree, until the assassins terror—the morning light, chased the murderers with their kindred fiends and the darkness to the abodes where the reveller in crime was the hero of the day.

Early in the morning of the 27th June, eventful day! A day ever to be remembered! The Prophet requested me to descend and interrogate the guard as to the cause of the intrusion upon us in the night, in doing which I was replied by the sergeant, whose name was Worrell, I think, of the Carthage Grays, in a very better spirit that "We have had too much trouble to bring old Joe here to let him ever escape out alive, and unless you want to die with him you better leave before sundown, and you are not a d-n bit better than him for taking his part." I endeavored to cool him down and to recall those threats which so ill became those who were entrusted with the lives of men, but he insisted the more "You'll see that I can prophesy better than old Joe that neither he nor his brother nor anyone who will remain with them will see the sun set today." With such threats did the Sergeant, in presence of his men, declaim against the prisoners: and one of them levelled and cocked his rifle at me, swearing with an awfull imprecation how he "would love to bore a hole through old Joe." Joseph and Hyrum were all this time listening unobservedly at the head of the stairs to all that was said, and on my return desired me to go and inform Governor Ford of all that I had heard.

While going to his Excellency's quarters I saw an assemblage of people and met Col. Markham who was out of the gaol before me; I listened to what they had to say and beheld one of the mobocrats addressing the crowd saying hat they would make a sham discharge in obedience to orders, but that the Gov. and MacDonough troops would leave for Nauvoo in the forenoon, "Then we will return to town boys and tear that prison down and have those two men's lives before sundown," which declaration was not uttered in a whisper nor in a corner, but at the top of his voice, which echoed in the walls of the Town Hall and public square, and which was responded to by the loud three cheers of the crowd as eagerly as [crease has worn away the words] another barrel of whiskey was called into their midst to the eternal disgrace of the name of sectarianism be it remarked. Accompanied by, whether Col. Markam, J. P. Green or J. S. Fullmore or who I do not remember, I went to His Excellency's apartment in Hamilton's Hotel, where I found several Officers with him in conversation; in their presence I informed him of the threats made against the lives of the prisoners, offering to produce further proof if necessary; to which he at length reply'd "You are unnecessarily alarmed for your friends safety Sir, the people are not that cruel." Irritated by such a remark I urged the necessity of placing better men than professed assassins to guard them; that they were American Citizens surrendered to his "pledged honour"; that they were also Master Masons, and as such I demanded the protection of their lives; when this appeal failed to reach his adamantine heart, whose face appeared to be pale with fright or horror, I remarked that I had then but one request to make if he left their lives in the hands of those men to be sacrificed. "What is that sir?" he asked in a hurried tone. "It is that the Almighty will preserve my life to a proper time and place to testify that you have been timely warned of their danger." All this produced no other visible effect than to turn him round and stroll to the other end of the room. I returned to the prison, and sought to enter, but would not be let in by the guard. I again returned to the Hotel when his Excellency was standing in front of the Mac Donough troops in line, ready to escort him to Nauvoo, the disbanded mob, retiring to their rear at the time, shouted loud in his hearing that they were going only a short distance out of town and would return and hang old Joe and Hyrum as soon as the Governor would be gone out of the way. I begged to call his attention there and then to their own threats which he could hardly fail to hear as well as myself [creased and worn line] for myself and friends to be in prison according to his promise to the prisoners when he declined giving any, but told Col. Demming to give me one to take to Dr. Richards the secretary, by obtaining which I was near being massacred, and was told by Chauncey Higbee on the street that they "were determined to kill Joe and Hyrum and that I had better go away to save myself." I was then alone in the midst of the turbulent mob with whom I contended for the innocency of the prisoners, and for their right of trial, until enraged, they attempted to seize me, but I eluded their grasp. Meeting Mr. A. W. Babbit in the street I informed him that Mr. Smith wished to see him, whither he went with me; he was admitted as Counsel. I tried to get in by means of Dr. Richards' pass, in my hand, but in vain; Joseph, Hyrum,—all endeavoured to get me in but failed; I however informed Dr. Richards who was allowed to come outside, of the threats of the mobs, who reply'd that they deemed my life in imminent danger in the midst of the mob. I was handed a letter from Mr. Smith, with a request to take it to Mr. Browning of Quincy forthwith; the guard aware of the letter informed the mob "that Joe had sent orders to raise the Nauvoo Legion to rescue him," drew the mob around me, and they demanded the letter, which I utterly refused to give up to them; when some would take it by force others objected; the mob disagreed among themselves while some said I should not leave the place alive, others swore that I should not stay longer there; at this the former party said if I left then I should not reach Nauvoo alive, and about a dozen started off with in hand to waylay me where the road runs through the woods. Having previously ordered my horse which was already in the street, I took advantage of their dis-agreement and no sooner in the saddle than both spurs were to work, and a racehorse and rider were enveloped in a cloud of dust with balls whistling nor saw the second scene until beyond the point of timber stretching into the prairie half a mile; to my right I discovered the road to Nauvoo, and the Gov. and escort about 4 miles off having dined there; proving that I was on the Carthage road, my horse having like myself, lost the waylaid road leading through the woods, and thereby escaped those awaiting me there. I turned across the plain to the order road, and passed the Governor, whereas, as was ascertained afterwards, had I advanced half a mile farther on the Carthage road, I should have come upon a gang of about 300 painted assassins who were then beyond a prairie ridge on that road waiting the disappearing of His Excellency in order to march upon the prison and execute the horrid threats. Thus I was providentially led as if between two fires unharmed. While tediously traversing the sea of grass which separated Nauvoo from Carthage, tho' under all the pressure my craft could carry, my dream in the prison came fresh to view, and this for the fulfillment of it;—the letter actually in my possession,—the troops in full view, myself going to Quincy filled my soul with ominous forebodings of the sequel, so that having left the troops far behind, arriving in the edge of the City I entreated of the crowds who had assembled to meet His Excellency to haste to Carthage and save the Prophet's life—the only alternative. But wiser ones, perhaps, had otherwise decreed, and I with thousands more had the mortification of seeing, formally, greeted within the mourning "City of Joseph" the "Pilate" that should have changed places and doom; had the untold disgrace I say of listening to a man stuck up in front of the Prophet's house, and harrangueing an innocent and inoffensive people with the insinuations applicable only to his own party; anything less than the superhuman endurance of those saints would have been tantalized to retaliate, when in presence of the wives, children, and friends of his victims he declared that "a great crime had been done by placing the City under Martial Law, [which was done only so far as self preservation from the mobs was demanding,] and a sever atonement must be made; so prepare your minds for the emergency." So awful a threat proceeding from the lips of the highest functionary of a State, while the victims had surrendered themselves as pledges of his "honour", drew from bursting hearts of many bystanders a half stifled shriek of horror as it echoed in the walls of the Prophet's house and drew louder shrieks from his wife and mother who later sank into her chair crying "My sons O my sons' lives are means to make the atonement." Even the obdurate spirit of the speaker felt the shock; and appeared to quiver from the effects of his own denunciations, from which he could not recoil. But I forbear to advert to that memorable oration! After which he and his escort were entertained at the Mansion House, and while sitting at the Prophet's table the hands of the assassins were dripping with his blood, and His Excellency might have said "A severe atonement has been made," as doubtless the Prophet and Patriarch were weltering in their own atoneing blood while their doom was being proclaimed to their families and friends.

Late that night I boarded a steamer bound to St. Louis, and landed at Warsaw after midnight, seeing a great excitement on the landing I stepped among them when I heard a mobocrat stating that "Joe and Hyrum were both shot while trying to escape from prison,"—He said that they had sent messengers to Quincy and the lower Counties to raise the Militia to defend Warsaw against an attack from the

Mormons: but that "their real object was, when they got them there, to take the beauty and booty of Nauvoo." One, in order to stimulate the others, said, "I know where a chest full of gold is hid in old Joe's cellar." The general feeling manifested there was of rejoicing at the crime committed, and of exulting in the horrid act shedding innocent blood, which reminded me of the sequel of my dream; altho' I hoped against hope that they boasted of their desires, rather than of overt acts. Then I got hold of a "Warsaw signal Extra," a slit of paper a little larger than my hand, was just issued, containing nothing but the news of the massacre; commencing by putting the letter J for Joe upside down; it stated "that the Mormons attacked the prison;—that the guards were compelled to shoot the prisoners in defense of their own lives, and to prevent their escape;—that three of the Citizens of Hancock were shot by Joe;— the Mormons have killed Governor Ford—and suite, burned Carthage; and we look for them to attack Warsaw every hour; will not the inhabitants of the surrounding Country rush to our defence before we, our wives and children will be massacreed." In order to dupe the public to believe this tissue of falsehood, without even a shadow of truth in one statement of it, to my positive knowledge, they had sent a number of women and children in their night clothes on a previous down Steamer to Quincy, merely to raise their sympathy in their favour, even when the mob acknowledged the whole as got up purposely to create alarm, and even boasted of "Tom Sharps" long headed shrewdness in the scheme, and exulted in the prospect of heralding forth that first impression on the public mind so as to justify the horrid deed; and singular as it may appear to a sane mind that the above account of the tragedy took the lead through all Newspapers through the States East, West, North & the Canadas, South & Texas, and then through Europe it went, thence around the world; and even to this day we find Clergy, Priests and Editors who either know no better, or knowing, willfully reiterate these glaring falsehoods to the ends of the Earth.

While on this passage down to Quincy 60 miles distant, I met a steamer crowded with soldiers and other passengers being the Militia first sent for by the mob to Warsaw,—the Boats neared and stopped; and to the disgrace of civilization, when the Captain of our boat reply'd to the enquiry for the news from above, "Nothing only old Joe and Hyrum are killed: "it was responded to by hearty cheers and swinging of hats by all that Boatfull of—what? As our passengers and crew had hats off to return the salute, I shouted at the top of my voice although inadvertently—"Shame Gentlemen, shame on such cruelty, will you by cheering approbate the blackest crime recognized by the law of even barbarous nations—will you as civilized men tolerate the cold-blooded murder of American Citizens, and that while laying in prison untried, while the honour of the State was pledged to protect them? Gentlemen desist, or whose lives will be safe if Republicanism is swallowed up by such a blood thirsty spirit as that? All this was spoken in much less time than writing and with other power than mine which carried shame to their faces, and paralized the arms that still clenched the hats tho' drooping by their sides, and sent them sneaking out of sight. On our arrival we saw the Carthage families in a crowd on the banks of the Mississippi as monuments of the sincerity of the blood stained crew, whose actions were admissable of the inefficiency of their testimonies to sustain their foul cause. Quincy was all in an uproar,—a crowd of Militia waiting for a steamer to take them to the scene of supposed action—the Warsaw mobs' emissaries inflaming the populace and distributing that infernal Budget of Tom Sharp the "Extra" already noticed. A meeting of the Citizens was convened in the City to which I repaired, and after listening to the death almost, to the exciting lies of the mob emmissaries of Warsaw—I jumped up and demanded a hearing—that I could prove all the statements made to be known falsehoods purposely to excite false alarm; a fuss followed "Down with him" Order, Order. "— "Hear the stranger;" the "Hear" carried and on I spun my tale; as if with a voice of fearless little thunder, characteristic of truth alone; I denied that the Mormon had attacked the prison, that I was the last Mormon but one from Carthage yesterday evening—left all the Mormons peacably at Nauvoo about midnight that Gov. Ford not any of his suit were neither killed nor wounded when they left Nauvoo early in the morning—that it was palpably false about Carthage being burnt;—that the Mormons had no intention of attacking Warsaw and that neither Militia nor any other need not trouble themselves about Warsaw or go there; unless they wished to attack Nauvoo, that was the only object mob had in calling them there; and I also told them what I had heard at Warsaw—carried a strong influence, and the Chair decided "No cause of alarm, all go about your business." Soon after this a Steamer came up the river having a company of Militia on board; again my antagonist mounted the wheelhouse and preached his infuriating sermon, who, before he could put in the amen, found another alongside of him tearing his B..cibw[sic] by piece meals, as he had done in the Court House, to his irremediable chagrin, and swayed a similar proselyting influence, so that instead of embarking more Militia on board, those already there landed and remained there. My noble friends (the mobocrats) just alluded to, forseeing the end of their campaigne in that field, concluded to leave on that Boat for Warsaw threatening veangeance on my head. Having accomplished my mission thereto, I was about going also had not the Captain of the Boat, who was an intimate friend of mine informed me that I had better wait for another Steamer, as the mobocrats had concocted a plan to take my life if I went up with them, to revenge on me for defeating their object. I accordingly waited till evening when I started up on another Boat. While on the passage, the hostile spirit of mobocracy was rife among the passengers, which caused much dispute because I would defend the innocency of Joseph and Hyrum; only occasionally I found a truth seeking person amongst them. Before we reached Warsaw the Captain and Clerk of the Boat, who were old friends of mine Boating together, informed me that some of the mob on board intend to inform at Warsaw that I was on board, and that "the mob there will take you ashore and hang you without Judge or Jury"—I remonstrated against going on shore, because if landed on the Illinois side I must travel up through the heart of a mob country who would hunt me out like hunting a wolf; whereas if I landed on the Missouri side it would be like jumping out of the frying pan into the fire. "—I could not escape them. They said that the fury of the mob was such that they would fire their cannons into the Boat, as they had done on other Boats bound for Nauvoo but they would do what they could. I told them I would risk the result with God if they would act up to my instructions which they promised to do; to the credit of Capt. Atchinson of the "Ohio" and generous Officers they did; for while the mob rushed on board as she landed crying "Where is Capt. Jones; where is he; bring him out; out with the d-d Mormon;" and while I could hear a general hallooing on shore "Bring him out, hang him up" &c., and I had crawled under a mattress alongside of which many more laid on the Cabin floor owing to the crowded state of the passengers, the Captain and Officers stood like lions in the Cabin floor keeping a drove of wolves from a pet lamb, declaring that they had landed me below the town. Turned off thus the mob returned on shore and back again only to be repelled the second time, while the mate was busily landing what freight they had for the place, the Engineer being ready to start by the sound of the bell for which I listened with breathless silence, nor dared to breath freely until the signal bell rang, and the Boat pushed off; nor did I regret to hear the mob plunge into the river splash,—splash after each other making for the shore without their prey, to the great disappointment of hundreds of blood thirsty mobs on shore, who had prepared a gallows on a tree on the bank and eagerly anticipated seeing the morning sun shine on a Mormon suspended by it. Fairly afloat—the God of my Salvation received the tribute of a grateful heart. I particularize on these scenes to illustrate the spirit prevalent amongst the mobocrats generally which seemed to sanction by their toleration the sacrifice of the lives of the Martyrs for the Gospel's sake; and altho' alone in this scene, surely I will be an incompromising witness against them.

In the forenoon I landed at the welcome shore of Nauvoo, but Oh what a scene! Never to be pictured or painted by the pencil of art! Sad as the tombs, cheerless groups mourning wend their way by closed stores and windows of former busy life towards the place where lay the bloody cor[p]ses of the martyrs! Old, young, male and female together bewail the day—their much loved Prophet and Patriarch from their embraces by ruthless assassins were untimely torn—how can they be comforted? The Sun and the Moon of the City's moral hemisphere are untimely set behind a cheerless bank of storm clouds. The wonted buoyant atmosphere seemed impregnated with death by suffocation—nor could heaven maintain its usual smiles; its face it vailed, and commiserating wept a shower of tears to comingle with those of the Saints below. Heart rending as was the scene beggar description until within the dining room of the Mansion House, statue like I stood, and saw in their coffins on tables laid the Prophet and Patriarch! Ah yes, fond hope no longer found a place to doubt, they are they—the lips from whence flowed the words of life like rivers that quenched the thirsting souls of thousands are closed in death—those eyes, the heaven lit torches, are dim and motionless, the spirit has fled. At the head of the one, bathed in tears, was seen the wife of the Prophet with her little boys and adopted Julia—at the other no less so was the Patriarch's wife surrounded by six little children who alternately with the grey haired Mother while kneeling in a pool of the comingling dripping gore of the Martyrs on the floor, with her streaming eyes first on one, then on the other cry "My husband, my husband too." "My father in blood". "And my father is dead too," and "My son, my sons" were the pitiful murmurings of the anguished widows and orphans that echoed in the walls which as but yesterday danced at the music of the Prophet's voice. On, on in solid columns the moving throng moved steadily to and off the solemn scene to take the last long look on those they loved most dearly—like the inexhaustible current of the mighty "Father of waters" as it for ages flows to the ocean appeared the passing current of mourning friends. The holes of the bullets, the bleeding gashes of the fatal bayonet need not the finger to point them out; nor need the assembled millions as[k] Who are they? When their "Elder Brother" from them will be distinguished by the prints of the nails in his hands and feet. But why linger o'er the horrid scene of humane fiendish conduct they are free, the Prophet and Patriarch have soared on high beyond the rage of mobs, their testimony sealed with their hearts blood when they could have escaped if they would, but heroic like demi-gods they firmly trod the road to death and glory; they boldly leaped on the scaffold with eyes open and souls unsullied—forever honoured be their memories. (Daniel Jones to Thomas Bullock, 20 January 1855, reprinted in *BYU Studies*, Vol. 24, No. 1, pg. 95-108)

# About the Author

Ted Gibbons was born and raised in Logan, Utah. After serving a mission to Brazil, he attended Utah State University on a theater arts scholarship. He graduated with a degree in both speech and education. In 1968 he married the former Lydia Kimball, then was inducted into military service. He was the Distinguished Military Graduate of his class, and after two years he reached the rank of captain.

Ted returned from the service to enter BYU to begin a Masters program, and after one term was hired by the Church Educational System to teach seminary in Phoenix. During three years at Arizona State University, he completed his Masters in audio visual education and was transferred to Snowflake, Arizona where he served as seminary principal for four years. In 1980, after returning from the Church Educational System's tour of Israel, Ted moved his family to Orem, Utah, where he began work on a Doctoral degree in Instructional Science at BYU. After two years in Orem on sabbatical and teaching at BYU, he was assigned to teach seminary at Pleasant Grove High School. He became principal there and later at MountainView Seminary in Orem. He is presently teaching at the Orem Institute of Religion.

In addition to his church assignments, he has participated for many years in the *Know Your Religion* program. He has presented hundreds of times over the past several years his one-man stage presentation of *Sealing the Testimony: Willard Richards' Eyewitness Account of the Martyrdom*. He is a published author of numerous books and articles, and was the co-lyricist of *Rabboni* an Easter cantata performed by the Tabernacle Choir.

Ted and his wife, Lydia, are the parents of twelve children.